THE
RIPTIDE

THE

RIPTIDE

The Untold Stories from Those Who Built the Alabama Dynasty

by

Jacob M. Carter

WordCrafts

TABLE OF CONTENTS

Dedication

This book is dedicated to everyone who has helped me achieve my dreams along the way. You are the riptide behind any success I have.

I love you all.

Soli Deo Gloria

Why did I Write This Book?

One day, while watching ESPN's *30 for 30* documentary on the USC dynasty, the idea for this book hit me. USC had a great run in the early to mid 2000's and they deserved all of the attention they were receiving on the show, but Alabama's dynasty was the greater story; at least in my opinion. After watching the show, I found myself wondering why there weren't more documentaries about the Crimson Tide's historic run. I was afraid that nobody would attempt to capture that run while it was fresh in the players' minds.

I decided I would attempt to capture it myself. I've never regretted that decision. I've enjoyed meeting a lot of former players and have even gained some friends along the way.

There are plenty of opinions swirling around about Alabama's football program in general, and Coach Saban in particular. This book is not an attempt to add my opinions to the pot. Instead, much like the *30 for 30* documentary on USC, I wanted to allow the players to tell their stories about the Alabama dynasty through their own personal experiences. I believe they enjoyed having that opportunity and I was blessed to learn from them as well.

I'm a life-long Alabama fan. I grew up during the "probation" years, when Alabama football was known more as a fossil than anything else. I recall, as a young boy, sitting in the sleet and rain in 2000, watching Alabama lose to their archrival Auburn - capping off a disappointing 3-8 season. It was tragedy in motion. I didn't think it could get worse... but it did.

Alabama, for most of my teenage years, was mired in mediocrity. They suffered from the repercussions of NCAA probation violations, and they shuffled head coaches in and out at an alarming pace. For a young Alabama fan, it was tough to endure. I had grown up hearing about the glory days of Bear Bryant and I was enamored with the Crimson Tide.

There was always something special about being around the stadium in Tuscaloosa for me. But those probation years seemed to wash that excitement away. By the time I was 18, I started to question whether

Alabama would ever rise up out the pit they were in.

But rise they did!

They not only rose up, they elevated their game beyond the fans' wildest imaginations.

If you didn't grow up in Alabama, or you haven't experienced what it's like to be part of the Crimson Tide culture, this might sound a little crazy to you. But Alabama fans are different. We take the wins and losses personally. We don't just go to the games; we live them. There's a hunger inside of us to see the Tide win championships.

Maybe it's because Alabama is the greatest dynasty of all time and it's just in our blood to carry that tradition forward. Maybe it's because we were raised to cheer for the Crimson and White and it would be treason to not do so with the highest expectations. Whatever the reason for our fanaticism, Alabama football is a part of us. It's a *Crimson* thing. And we wouldn't have it any other way.

Which brings me to the real reason I wrote this book. I wanted my favorite program, which has given me so many personal moments of joy in my life, to be represented like the USC program was in that ESPN documentary. I wanted dedicated fans, like myself, to be able to experience this historic run through the eyes of those who lived it. I wanted the University of Alabama, Coach Saban and the players to know how much the fans appreciate all of their hard work. We want to pay it forward to them as much as we can.

I wanted the fans to know how much love the players have for them. I wanted a young prep prospect to know what it is that separates Alabama from every other college football program in the country.

The Alabama Crimson Tide is in the midst of a special time in college football history. As they continue to shred the record books, they also have set a standard for the rest of the world to adore. They do things the right way; they do it with class. Why wouldn't I want to share that story with anyone and everyone I could?

Roll Tide!

Introduction

Amongst the calm beauty and glamour of the sea there is danger, a hidden undercurrent, strong enough to sweep away anything it comes into contact with. It is deceptive; a calm stream that runs through the midst of waves, lulling unsuspecting swimmers into the mistaken belief that is the safest spot to frolic. This is a fatal mistake, for this undercurrent grabs a man, wears him down, leeches away his strength through its constant, relentless flow of water that surrounds him, tugs him, pulls him out to sea. It is unsuspecting. It is remorseless. It is powerful. This is the riptide.

Alabama football, commonly referred to as the Crimson Tide, is such a force. There are many legends from Tuscaloosa who have made appearances on national television and graced the front covers of magazines. Those players deserve every accolade they have achieved. They are the face of the program. But there is another group of lesser-known names that have been the backbone of Alabama's recent dynasty. These players represent what I call the *Riptide* of the dynasty.

Like the riptides of the ocean, they are often unheralded, yet they have had a fatal impact on Alabama's opponents. They are the missing link of the Alabama story that needs to be told. They are the scout players, the fullbacks, the grind workers who don't look for the recognition they deserve. They are the guys who push their teammates during the week to prepare for the war on Saturday. They make key blocks to free up lanes for running backs. They produce big hits in game changing situations. They answer when they're called upon to score a touchdown in crunch time. They sweep away their competition and never say a word about it.

I wanted to write this book to give these Riptide players a voice. I wanted people to understand how vital they have been to the overall success of Alabama's modern dynasty.

I was personally impacted by how important every player of Alabama's team really is in regards to them pushing one another in every aspect of the game. Let me give you some examples. Courtney Upshaw, the former highly-decorated Alabama linebacker, needs a Ben Howell to push him in practice so Upshaw can perform at a high level once he's in the game. Without former Crimon Tide running back Roy Upchurch, maybe there is no Mark Ingram because of the mentorship Upchurch was able to bring to a young Mark when he arrived in Tuscaloosa. Eryk Anders had to fight for his spot as a linebacker, but he eventually won it over and sealed the deal for Alabama in the National Championship in 2009. Parker Philpot walked on at Alabama and played his role without complaining. He pushed the starters to greatness day in and day out in the summer and fall camps through his determined commitment to Coach Saban's process. Parker is a two-time National Champ. There are many more stories just like these throughout this book. I hope you're starting to grasp the importance of these Riptide players when it comes to winning football games in T-Town.

We live in a culture that promotes the individual. We see the star quarterbacks and flashy wide receivers and we end up leaving the roots of what works best in life in the first place - teamwork. I've sat back as a fan for years and watched Alabama systematically dismantle teams through an old-school team mentality. It's been beautiful. We look at Coach Saban and all of the hype surrounding the program and we sometimes forget that none of the things they have accomplished came without the sacrifice of the next man beside them.

The players on Alabama, from the stars to the walk-ons, sacrifice their egos and personal agendas for the overall success of the program. This doesn't just happen. It's against our human nature to be that selfless. Coach Saban leads this selfless philosophy by example, and that example bleeds over onto the rest of his team. All of this is done with consistency and the results are stunning. Alabama has won four National Championships in less than a decade. In today's culture of "I," that is an incredibly difficult thing to do.

This is the story of how some of the lesser-known names helped the Alabama Crimson Tide rise from the ashes of despair to once again rule college football. Coach Nick Saban and his staff have built an amazing system that has not been duplicated. They cannot be denied. Yet, they have also been able to recruit some amazing young men to drive that system to near perfection. The Riptide of Alabama's program has silently swept away the bitter years of probation through their self-determined attitude to not be denied for the sake of their brothers, on and off the field. In short, these guys, like their head coach, chose to sacrifice their names for the sake of being a part of something special.

How did they do it? How did they stay so consistent? What are the fundamentals of the dynasty? I think it's time I turn the reader over to the players themselves so you can grasp Alabama's program at a deeper level than you ever have before.

Eryk Anders

Eryk Anders is a former linebacker at Alabama and was a starter on the 2009 National Championship team. His roots are in San Antonio, Texas, where he was an All-State player at Smithson Valley High School.

Eryk is famous these days for his fighting skills inside the world of Mixed Martial Arts. (He's a trainer at Spartan fitness in Homewood, Alabama.) He's also a legend at Alabama because of his role on the 2009-10 National Championship team. With the clock running out against Texas, Eryk sped around the end of the line and forced a game clinching fumble when he sacked Longhorn Quarterback Garret Gilbert.

I loved talking with Eryk, because he is full of heart about the Alabama program. He really put a taste in my mouth for how Coach Saban's program becomes a part of those who play for him. Eryk spoke as if his experiences at Alabama shaped and molded him as the husband and father he is today. He also gave me an understanding of how hard a linebacker has to work at Alabama to even compete on the scout team, much less start for the Crimson Tide in a title game. Eryk personifies what this book is about. He is a selfless player who simply "does his job."

How were you apart of the Alabama football program?

Well, I was a starter on the '09 National Championship team. I had back up roles and special team roles up until then. In the 2008 season, I would come in on obvious passing situations, third and long, second and long. You know, I was trying to put some pressure on the quarterback. I found a great deal of success doing that. My senior year, 2009, I was able to win a starting spot.

Were you recruited by Nick Saban to Alabama?

No, I was recruited by the Shula administration.

Was it a culture shock when Nick Saban took over for Mike Shula?

More of us was demanded under Coach Saban. I will say this, Shula's practices were a bit harder, but Saban brought the NFL approach, you know, a lot of meeting times and things like that. We didn't beat each other up so much in practice. Tuesdays and Wednesdays were our hitting days, and we had Mondays off with Coach Shula, but Coach Saban wasn't having any of that.

There are a lot of opinions that swirl around about who Nick Saban is. What do you think is something people don't know about Coach Saban or his program?

He doesn't demand anything out of his players that he doesn't demand out of himself, or his coaching staff. So, for example, they are up there from six in the morning till ten at night. There's no way the players could do that, obviously, because of class schedules and NCAA rules for how long practices can go and players can actually be up there. A lot of people don't understand the devotion he has to the Crimson Tide, and to the sport of football in general.

Is Coach Saban intimidating?

I wouldn't say he's intimidating. I guess he intimidates some people, but other people aren't. I guess that's a personal thing, I would say. He's very demonstrative though, I will say that.

With the legacy that Alabama carries in regards to a stingy defense, what kind of mindset does a defensive player have under Coach Saban? Is that mindset developed over time, or does it come along with the territory?

Well, I think it kind of just goes with the Alabama stigma. You know, we have had two Heisman trophy winners, and it's the defense that keeps the offense on the field, if you will. It gives the offense the opportunity to put up numbers, and rack up points. Alabama's always had a good defense, and will always have a good defense, especially under Saban, and especially now that he's getting the recruits that he wants. He's been able over the last seven years to implement his game plan. When we were there he came in when I was a redshirt sophomore. So, there was a bit of an adjustment period. Now, guys are coming in, and they're going straight into his system so the defense is going to get better and better.

What is Nick Saban's process?

He wants you in shape mentally and physically. A lot of people think the game of football is a physical game, but it's just as much mental as it is physical. So, he puts you through conditioning tests and strength and conditioning programs that really bring you to your mental breaking point. When it's over you breathe that sigh of relief because he tends to make practice more intense than what you would see in a real game. For instance, we run like a 100-120 plays per practice, when the average number of plays run per game is 70 or 80. Practices are definitely more intense than the game. A lot of times we're not trying to beat each other up, and hurt each other so we can be healthy for the game. But mentally those practices are a lot more strenuous. He puts us in situations where you're almost set up to lose, so he definitely has that part of the game figured out.

What is the fourth quarter program?

We run 110-yard sprints, and he breaks us up into three groups, according to position. You have the big guys, the offensive linemen and the defensive linemen. The mid-scales, your linebackers and tight ends, and your skills positions - you know, your running backs, wide receivers, cornerbacks and safeties, and guys like that. Each group has a certain time they have to make, otherwise it doesn't count. I mean we had to run 110 yards 16 times in under 15 seconds. If someone ran it in like 16 or 17 seconds, that rep doesn't count, and everybody has to do another one. His first year there, we were only supposed to do 16 and we ended up doing 39 of them because people were missing their time, or someone was bent over or looked tired, so they added another one and another one and another one and we eventually got to 39 before we did them all correctly.

What were some of your favorite experiences as a player at Alabama?

It was definitely game time. Right before a game and right after the game. During the game, it's kind of a blur because it's moving so fast and things are just happening like boom, boom, boom, boom. After the game, celebrating the victory with the people you bled with and sweated with. The camaraderie of the locker room, especially during the 2009-year, was unbelievable. There are guys, you know, I haven't spoken to in years, but when I see them at the Alabama spring game we pick up right where we left off. So, I think that right there was my favorite part of playing at Alabama. You know, it was the brothers that I made, and the camaraderie in the locker room.

Do you have a particular game that you played in that sticks out in your mind?

It was definitely the Texas game. That game in the National Championship was probably the best game that I had all year statistically. I had the big play at the end that kind of put the ball back in the hands of the offense. And, I'm from Texas. I wasn't recruited by Texas, but we played Texas. You know, I grew up ninety miles south of Austin, where the University of Texas is, so it was a great feeling to get that win. Not only to get the win, but also to play them in the Rose Bowl which is widely seen as the most prestigious bowl game of them all. To have such a good game personally, with a sack and a forced fumble at the end of the game to put the ball back into the hands of the offense to kind of seal the win gave me a hell of a moment.

Also, the Florida game. Florida had beaten us the year before, and they went on to win a National Championship that year. You know, that put such a bitter taste in my mouth the whole season, and we beat them. Then, to cap it off with the win over Texas in the Championship, you know, you couldn't script it any better for me personally.

Could you walk us through your game clinching sack in the 2009 National Championship game?

That play was actually an audible. A lot of people don't know about Coach Saban and the complexities of his defense. It's run just like an offense. Every play had two or three changes built into it, so we can call the original play and if someone motions one way or another, depending on the game plan, the defensive play can change. On that particular play we had a different defense called, and the audible was if they came out in empty backfield with five wide that we would audible where I would rush off the edge. They came out five wide. There were three on my side and two on the other side. I lined up on the third receiver closest to the offensive tackle, and I kind of showed that I was in pass coverage. As I was looking in I noticed that the offensive tackle wasn't even looking at me. You know, he was looking down towards the interior lineman, I believe it was Marcell Dareus, so I knew that I was going to come free.

I'm out there shadowing on the third receiver, I believe it was Shipley, I can't remember. Which, I don't know how they fell for that because obviously you're not going to put a linebacker on Shipley. Anyway, they saw the blitz coming from the other side and shifted the protection that way, and at the snap I got on my horse and took off running. Garret Gilbert's back were to me. I actually thought he had thrown the ball because he pump-faked it, and hid it, but you know, I thought in my head, "I'm here now, so let's see what happens and I'm glad I didn't pull up because he definitely had the ball in his hands when I hit him I looked up I saw everybody running the other way, and then I saw Courtney Upshaw jump on the ball. I don't get excited much, I'm not an emotional person, but I was pretty ecstatic at that moment.

What was it like to win a National Championship at Alabama?

I'm not sure there are words in the English dictionary to describe the feeling. You know, Alabama has such a rich tradition of winning - not just winning, but winning championships - and to be on the team, and play a starting role on the team that got Alabama back on track kind of resonates with me. It was great to get the Tide rolling once again.

Due to the sports culture in Alabama, do you think that going to school there made more of a long-term impact on you?

No question, and I don't think that too many people can deny the loyalty in the fan base of Alabama. It is one of the best, if not the best fan base in all of college football. There are people elsewhere in the country that can't even point out Tuscaloosa on the map, yet they're big time Alabama fans. I don't think there are a whole lot of schools in the country that are like that. You know, Alabama is just good like that.

How do you think going to Alabama affected your life?

I got my college degree, and having a college degree really sets you up for success. And just the mental fortitude that you develop with the program at Alabama really helps you deal with all of the ups and down that life can throw at you.

If you had a young recruit sitting in front of you, why would you encourage him to go to Alabama?

If you want to win, the statistics speak for themselves. Four out of the last seven championships have come underneath Nick Saban. He's won elsewhere too, so he's a proven winner. If you do what you're supposed to do and trust in the process, and have a decent season, you're going to have a chance to play in the NFL. If you don't, at least you're going to walk away with a college degree, which is going to set you up for the future. I strongly suggest it. I would say something along those lines.

How important is the player's education to Nick Saban and his staff?

He definitely stresses getting an education and getting your degree. He has a saying that nobody's better off without their degree than they are with it. You know, I think he has like an eighty-five or ninety percent graduation rate and the other guys that don't graduate leave and go to the NFL. So, the opportunity is there to make it to the next level. It's just really up to you to trust the process, and do what you're supposed to do on your end, and he's going to do what he's supposed to do on his end, and he's proven that time and time again with his success and his graduation rate at the University of Alabama.

Where does the 2009 team rank in the Saban dynasty?

Um, it's definitely in the top two. The 2011-2012 defense was also stingy, but I think the '09 team was great. Especially because a lot of the players on that team weren't Coach Saban's. A lot of them were Coach Shula's recruits, so he was able to take the people who wouldn't have necessarily been in his system and turn them into an efficient group. We became very efficient in what we did, and I just think that '09 team is a special group. There's a lot about that team that other teams can't duplicate. We went through a lot of diversity with the coaching change, and it was a much more difficult task. Now, they expect to win all the time and the fans expect them to win all the time, so there was no expectation for our team. Everyone made excuses for us because we had a new coach and a new system, so I just think there's something special about that team.

How good was Mark Ingram, the first ever Heisman trophy winner at Alabama, in practice?

To be 100 percent honest with you, and I think every guy on that '09 defense will tell you the same thing; everybody knew Mark was a special football player, there's no doubt about that, but everybody also knew that Eddie Lacy was going to be the man one day. You know, he had some injuries while he was in school, but now he's in the NFL and he's certainly proving that fact.

What's it like to practice against such elite athletes, day in and day out at Alabama?

At Alabama when you line up against the guy next to you, there's a pretty good chance he's the best in the country at what he does. He's at least in the top five. The offense is practicing against one of the best defenses and the defense is practicing against one of the best offenses so it's not like there's a shock and awe when you go up against other teams because generally they're not as prepared as you are or the guy that you practice up against all week. Alabama definitely has a leg up in that department as well.

When Nick Saban says not to look at the scoreboard and to do your job, what does he mean by that?

I came from a really good high school team, and that was preached to me in high school, so I was glad to have someone rehashing that in college in well, because some of these guys don't come from that background. One thing Coach Saban early on talked about was playing three teams; LSU, Auburn, and I forget the third team, but they were the three biggest threats in the SEC, and then we turned around and lost to Louisiana Monroe. At the end of the season, Coach called the players into his office and kind of has a conversation with us. I remember he asked me what changes, if any, should be brought to the team, or whatever. I brought up that my high school didn't bring up beating any one team more than we did the other, and I thought we had a pretty good season, so I told him the same thing that maybe we shouldn't talk one team more than another and we should just act like we were playing a big game every week, and the next season we went 12-2, and the next we went 14-0. I like to think I had something to do with that on the backend as well.

A lot of the media presents Nick Saban as a control freak and dominating taskmaster. Since you played for him, do you think those criticisms are unfair?

Absolutely. No one in the real world cares about excuses or what you have going on in your personal life, so he doesn't allow you to make excuses for yourself. That's just not practical to life. This is the task we have to do, and we're going to do it, and if you can't do it we will find someone who will. You can't act like a knucklehead and fail a drug test or not go to class. If you do act like one, you will be replaced until you get back on track and I think that's how the real world works.

So is his mindset the "tough love" mindset?

Yeah, I mean, this is what we're going to do and we have to do it. Period. If you don't want to be on board, we're going to find someone who is. Me, as a parent, I would rather send my child to play for someone like that rather than someone who will baby them. I feel like if you baby a child too much, it's not a good thing. So, he provides the exposure to some of the realities of the real world for young men without making excuses for them.

What is it like to run out of that tunnel on Saturday with 100,000-plus fans screaming for you in Bryant Denny stadium?

It's indescribable. You know, you run out of tunnel and the fans are screaming and all fired up. But, to me the best the best games were the away games because I love hostile situations. We played at LSU's stadium in 2008 and went to three overtimes and it was so loud in that stadium that I couldn't have a conversation without screaming at the top of my lungs. It was crazy how loud and amped up that stadium was. We got the win, but we had to keep our helmets on because of some of those crazy Louisiana fans. (Laughs) So for me personally, I love the hostile environments, and there's no stadium more hostile than Death Valley. But, the fans that are cheering for you is also an indescribable feeling on the other end. You know, there's just so much love and appreciation that Alabama fans put out towards the players and the coaching staff. I just don't think that kind of love is replicated anywhere else in the country.

Were you prepared for how big of a deal Alabama football was when you stepped on the campus?

Man, I had no idea what I was getting myself into. One of my high school coaches, Chris Robertson, told me I had no idea what I was getting myself into. The day I signed, I went over to Coach Robertson's house, and he told me I didn't understand the magnitude of the fans over there, and I was like "yeah right," so he went online and went to an Alabama forum and these people already knew more about me than I knew about myself. That was crazy. I get on campus, and students are approaching me, and older and younger people who knew who I was. I just thought it was nuts. After my first week on campus I called Coach Robertson, and told him it was unfathomable and he was right. They knew my stats, and everything about me.

Some people are turned off by that, and some really like that kind of attention. Which category did you fall in?

For me personally, I'm kind of a low-key person, so I didn't know how to act. I just kind of smiled and nodded my head and went about my way. You know, some guys really embrace that super-star status, but I was a fan of Barry Sanders growing up, and he was probably one of the humblest guys to ever play football, so I didn't know how to take it. I still don't know how to act when I introduce myself and people know my name. It's an unbelievable experience. It's hard to replicate anywhere else at a genuine level like it is here at Alabama.

What do you have to say about the Alabama dynasty? Are you surprised they have continued their success since you have left?

Not at all. After playing for Coach Saban for three years, I'm not shocked at all. When they lose a game, I'm like, what went wrong? I know how well prepared they are. I know the level of the athletes they bring in to the university so every time they win a championship I think it was a no-brainer. They will be in the title run every year that Coach Saban is there.

What do people not realize about the character of each team that plays under Nick Saban?

People think they know, but they don't know the amount of work and effort that goes into every practice, and watching film. A lot of guys are watching film on their free time too. I just don't think people understand what it takes. Only one percent of high school players end up playing college football and only 25 players out of that one percent will play for Alabama, so unless you're there doing it, you don't know.

Is Nick Saban the best Coach in college football?

It's hard to argue otherwise. I mean, four Championships in seven years. Also, the other teams that won the National championships in the years 'Bama didn't went through 'Bama - except for Florida State. All roads go through Alabama, especially now with the college football playoff system. Alabama is the gold standard in college football.

When you're older, how much will it mean to you to have been a part of the Alabama dynasty?

I'm very proud. I have a six-year-old son. You know, he's very proud. Anytime someone is around him he's always the first one to tell them that his daddy played for Alabama, his daddy won a championship at Alabama. He's only six, so when he's old enough to comprehend some of the war stories it's going to get even better.

What are you doing now in life?

I do mixed martial arts. I fight in the cage like you see on TV. I'm also a personal trainer at Spartan fitness in Birmingham, Alabama where I teach classes and also give private lessons.

Do you have any closing remarks about Alabama football?

Roll Tide!

Roy Upchurch

Roy Upchurch is a former Alabama running back who was part of the 2009 National Championship team. Roy played at Godby High School and was named a Parade High School All-American before he enrolled at Alabama. Roy's game winning catch against the Auburn Tigers in 2009 is arguably one the greatest moments in Iron Bowl history.

Roy Upchurch is a man of faith. He believes in himself and the people around him. He believes in perseverance and he lives that belief out by example. I wanted him to be a part of this project because he embodies the Riptide of Alabama's program. Roy came into Alabama's program during the transition from Coach Shula to Coach Saban. He humbled himself from having to be a star and matured into being a man. He led the other star running backs at Alabama, such as Mark Ingram and Trent Richardson, until the fruit of their labor was produced for the world to see. He was always there, lurking in the crimson waters, until he finally swept Auburn away by finishing them off with his game-winning touchdown in 2009.

Roy is now a trainer at South Carolina, but the Crimson Tide will always be a part of who he is. I hope that any Alabama fan who is about read this interview will pay close attention to the amount of selflessness an Alabama player must have in order for the entire team to see its vision fulfilled.

How were you a part of the Alabama football program?

I was recruited by Mike Shula. I was a four-star recruit out of Tallahassee, Florida. I was one of the top recruits in my class. Coach Shula told me I could come in and compete for a starting job, and that sold me to the University of Alabama. Originally, I was going to go to Arkansas, but Darren McFadden and Felix Jones had already committed, so I decided to go to Alabama.

What was the transition like for you when Coach Saban took over the head coaching position at Alabama?

You know, Coach Shula didn't have the aggressive approach. I won't say he didn't have the aggressive approach to win right now, but Coach Saban came in with the approach to better the program immediately. He wanted to implement the things that he had success with at LSU that had granted him a chance to win a championship. He brought those things there, and his motto was if you don't buy in, then he doesn't want you to be a part of his team. Everybody from the freshman to the fifth-year seniors started buying in, and accepted the new wave of coaching and the new wave of success. That was one of the things Coach Saban implemented at his arrival in Tuscaloosa.

Because you were a running back at Alabama, did their style of how they wanted you to perform change underneath Coach Saban's system?

Not really. Coach Saban and Coach Shula relied on running the football. They had a lot of success with Coach Shula running with Ken Darby. He was an all-SEC guy. The same success happened with Coach Saban with Glen Coffee and Mark Ingram, and the list goes on and on.; Derrick Henry and Eddie Lacy. They really believed that running the football wins football games. It takes away a big chunk of the ball game if you can run the football and control the clock.

What does a running back do in a day-to-day Alabama practice?

Under the direction of Burton Burns, we just emphasized being tough runners. We wanted to be downhill guys who punish anyone who comes in our way. You know, Coach Burns really emphasizes finishing runs down field and splitting safeties down the middle of the field. He really preached a lot about making one cut and then getting vertical. That's one thing I implement as well, being a coach now. They like an every-down back; a guy who can keep going; a guy who could take 30 to 40 carries; a guy who can run for 2,000 yards, as we saw this year. They just want a guy who really can work hard and carry the team.

What is the process of Nick Saban's program?

The process starts, of course, with being accountable in the classroom. If you're not accountable in the classroom, you basically forfeit your scholarship. And then it bleeds onto the field where you have to dedicate your mind, body and everything you got to the program, the football training facilities, and to the coaches as well. If it's running 110s, you have to give all you got. You have to strain. You have to be able to endure and surpass the workload that they're throwing on you. Just as far as the heavy weights you lift; the heavy back squats. You know, you have to able to outlast the program just to be successful.

When Coach Saban preaches about not looking at the scoreboard, people perk their ears. Was that a hard mindset for you to adopt once he got there?

I think when he tells us, *"don't look at the scoreboard,"* it's just a mindset of really dominating your opponent and not giving up. Don't even let your opponent have a breath of air. That's why we train so hard. That's why the practices are so hard. Tuesday and Wednesday practices are like NFL practices in my eyes. You have to be able to sustain the hard work. Coach Saban really harps on not watching the scoreboard just because it's just a mindset of finishing the game. If you do what you're supposed to do and not look at the scoreboard you're going to dominate your opponent for so many plays that it's going to be routine, and it's going to become easier and easier and easier each opponent that you play. I think that mindset really just allows guys to focus in on each play and allow each play to be a breath of life on its own. Once you get that mentality and once you program that into your head, guys become unstoppable. They can be in position to run the ball 40 times a game and rush for almost 300 yards, or make eight tackles or just outlast their opponent. When you take away the scoreboard factor, it becomes basically a boxing match.

Nick Saban's first year at Alabama ended with a 7-6 record. The next season you guys finished 12-2, and the year after that you were the undefeated National Champions. What was the climb to the top like?

The year we went 7-6 was a growing year for us, and especially my class. You know, we were the younger, more experienced guys, who were the next guys up to potentially bring the championship or potentially change the program and once everybody bought in we started seeing glimpses of success.

The 7-6 year was a very hard year. That year we lost to Louisiana Monroe. It was just an eye opener. We look back on Coach Saban's success and he never had those types of seasons, and for us as players we wanted to be accountable to him and respect him and just accept everything the he ascribed to us to become champions. That season was the turning point where we all kind of saw the light and locked in and thought we could be great.

The next year we ended up going to the SEC championship, and if it wasn't for a pass interference play I believe we would have gone to the national championship that year. The growth just continued year after year after year, and guys started believing in themselves and the program.

All the irrelevant guys were excused from the program or dismissed, so you had a bunch of winners and guys who wanted to have success. That following year when we won the championship we had a team full of guys who just wanted to be the best as a person and as a football player. They wanted to accomplish something they never had in their lives.

You know, people dream of winning a National Championship, and to accomplish that was such an elating situation. It brought success to the program and success amongst others. Year after year guys are starting to get that winning mentality. Recruits are going to the best school because they know how to create champions. Being at Alabama unlocked so much of a potential champion in myself as well as many, many others. I just really think that Coach Saban's system is flawless if you just accept the things that he really has planned.

What do you think people don't know about Nick Saban?

That he's a great guy. You know, you see him have some tirades on TV, and get upset, but he's not that type of guy. He's the type of guy that will sit down and talk to you, and really try to figure you out, to better you as an individual. He's the type of guy that can unlock a whole lot of potential in you. He's the type of guy that you can learn who he is and apply it to yourself and almost become as much of a perfectionist as he is. You can just learn from the routineness of his life and the steps he takes to put others in position to have success. A lot of people don't know he can unlock so much potential in a person.

Is Nick Saban's job bigger to him than just winning football games?

Oh, it's way bigger. He wants to see players not only develop as great athletes, but also great student-athletes. He wants to see people have a great future. He wants to see his athletes walk across the stage. He wants to see his University's graduation rate go up. You know, I think football is smaller in his eyes than what he wants for student-athletes. He wants them to become good men in life. He wants his guys to be good fathers. He wants them to represent his family's last names as well in an awesome manner.

The whole experience at Alabama will open guys so they can unlock their potential and accomplish those things. They can graduate, and even move on to the next level, even if it's not in the NFL. You know, I had the opportunity to just try out, and I didn't make it, but I remember so many days where I spoke with Coach Saban and he told me I was talented in other ways. That unlocked so much potential in me, and him helping me has made me a successful coach and a great dad and a great mentor that people can believe in.

What kind of impact did playing at Alabama have on your life?

I think it made me grow into a man a little faster because coming in I would say I was a little immature. But with the assistance of Coach Burns, and Coach Saban, and even guys like Jeff Allen, those guys unlocked my potential. I wasn't a Heisman trophy winner, but they pushed me every single day to be the best person, to graduate, and to show up on the field. Now that I look back on it, I feel like those guys really helped my experience. Now that I'm a father, today I know the things I need to teach my child in how to be successful in the things he wants to put his mind to. I even feel like with my four-year-old son I ascribe a championship mentality the same way Coach Saban did with us. I've understood what it takes to overcome adversity in life, in football, in careers, and I continue to have success by continuing on. Those guys taught me how to continue to fight and never lay down and never give up on the things I want for myself and for my family.

Let's shift gears a little. You were a part of arguably one of the greatest running back trios in the history of college football. That backfield included Heisman trophy winner Mark Ingram, and eventual Heisman trophy finalist, Trent Richardson. What was it like to be apart of that group?

Sharing the backfield with these guys was a great opportunity. One reason is because I took a backseat to their success, and also kind of helped critique those guys on the field as far as how to see things, and how to see the hole and speed in and out of it. I think it was a learning experience for me. Just to see those guys have success when they were that young, it just really showed that they're really talented backs. It kind of made us all want to eat and compete against each other.

Everyday at practice we would hold each other accountable to just give your heart. Go out there and drain every ounce you had to just get better so everybody can be on the same page and work as hard as the next man. That ignited the creation of those two. It was the hard work and the grind. It was us pushing each other to the max each day. Even with Eddie Lacy on the rise - you know, he was another guy who helped push us and create a mindset that we were the best.

I remember when we played Clemson in '08 for the first game. A lot of that showed and then in '09 those guys just turned into complete monsters. They came in and they never took a rep off in practice, and in game situations it was almost easy. I think it was just the hard work and dedication that we put in that helped the guys reach the level of success that they achieved.

What was it like for you to lower your head and enforce your will on a would-be tackler?

It's all about setting the tone. You know, if you impose fear in your opponent, they're not going to try to come up and tackle you the next time. They're going to think about it. Our mentality was to go out there and set the tone. Run somebody over. Stiff-arm somebody. Crack-back somebody. Make somebody pay to set the tone for your team. That's one way I channeled my energy. I always wanted to set the tone. I played very little, but when I made a play I always wanted to make an impact. I would tell myself everyday, "steal the show". Make a big play. Make a crack-back block for Javier in the Iron Bowl. I was programmed to make an impact in any way possible. I wanted to impose my will on my opponent, and just go out there and have fun and make them pay.

RIPTIDE

Was the 2009 National Championship team an unselfish group?

I don't think the '09 team was selfish at all. We all bought into the program. Everybody started seeing that everyone was having success and everyone wanted a piece of the pie. Even when Mark would get dinged up, Trent would step in, or I would come in and step in. Even when we were up by two touchdowns, the younger guys would come in and dominate just as efficiently as the first team. Guys would have big plays, and big runs and that's a very unselfish mentality. That goes back to buying in.

That type of unselfishness creates that championship mentality. Everybody wanted to see everybody do so well. You know, the first string was excited our third and fourth string guys were getting in because they were the future. You want to see what the future looks like when you're having success. I really think that team was locked in on not being a selfish team, of not being a stat-keeper. The guys didn't poke their chest out if they scored three or four touchdowns. Everybody believed in a *team* win, and that's why we had so much success.

What is it that people don't know about playing running back?

I think one of the things that people don't see is that you always have to make your lineman correct. You always press the line of scrimmage just to make the pieces of the puzzle go together. There's five linemen, plus you, but you have to make the lineman correct. You have to complete the task at hand that they're asking you to do. It's just like if a receiver has to run a three-yard slant at the correct depth to make the piece of the puzzle go with the play.

I think at the running back position you have to do your assignment, and set your runs up to where your linemen are always correct. That's one thing Coach Burns really taught us. Another thing is that you have to have good vision and good acceleration. It really comes down to heart in the end. You have to have the will to finish games, and impose your will. You have to sacrifice for the team. Just the position alone takes a lot of heart to play.

One the greatest moments in Iron Bowl history was when you caught the potential game-winning touchdown pass from Greg McElroy in 2009. Could you break that play down for us?

I'm not sure what play was called before. I get close to the headset and yell, *"let's go "Cody 5."* into the headset. That was a personnel formation where Terrence Cody and I go into the game, and it's basically just like a run power play action. So, we sell the power and there's a play action right off of it. Mark was out, so Trent was carrying the workload in the fourth quarter during that drive and he needed a break. I was on the sideline, just anxious to go in the game. Coach Saban took a timeout right before he called the play. My job was to bluff the defensive end and escape to the flats. I mean, we practiced the play all year, but we never called it or had a game time situation so close where we needed to call it. I believe it was the perfect call.

It's funny because I went and saw Jim McElwain down in Florida a couple of months ago and he always tells me that he can never forget that I helped him call that play. It was a great feeling just to have that success and that vision as a coach. Just to call something in that situation and to go out and execute it as well was amazing. It was a great play designed by Coach McElwain, and I really just think I was at the right place, at the right time.

Could you describe the feeling of playing in the Iron Bowl?

The rivalry in the Iron Bowl is just bragging rights for the state. You know, you work so hard just to be the best in the country as well as in the state, I look back as a freshman in college, and Tommy Tuberville was the coach at Auburn and we had lost like five straight, and I remember "The Thumb" and how much slander we took at Alabama just because they were on top and the rivalry was very heated.

When Coach Saban arrived everybody kind of bought into the rivalry even more. Just playing in the Iron Bowl is amazing. You know, I just hear stories about it from Bo Jackson and Cam Newton and guys who have gone on and played elite football. I think it's a phenomenal rivalry and it goes back for years. That's one game in the state and in the country that people look forward to just because it's so deep with tradition. You know, I'm from Florida, so it took me a while to adapt to the rivalry. But, once I understood it, it was like going to war for your state and putting on for Alabama.

What was your favorite moment at Alabama?

One of them was Mark Ingram winning the Heisman Trophy. I sat back and watched this kid emerge from a three-star athlete to winning to the Heisman Trophy; the first Alabama player to ever win the Trophy. Just watching him have that success was... I was just so happy for the kid. I was happy to just be on the same team as him, and have a relationship with him.

Another was of course the National Championship. I had dreamed about winning a National Championship every since I was about 12 or 13 years old. Everybody can't say they will go to college and win one, but years ago I kind of felt like I would one day, but I never knew when. That was an amazing moment in my Alabama career.

Also, my catch in the Iron bowl. That will never be forgotten, and I really appreciate the fans for just allowing me to be apart of the Alabama family and to represent everybody well and to go out and put it all on the line for the state of Alabama and the University of Alabama.

I love being apart of the SEC. It's a phenomenal conference and it's great competition. It's almost like the baby NFL. In the end, just coming and working with my coaches and being a part of it; seeing my teammates have success and being a part of it. That's the appreciation of just everybody buying into the program.

When you're older and you look back on this run, what will it mean to you that you were apart of the Alabama dynasty?

It will mean a lot. To be able to sit and tell my son stories about how great this team was, you know, from Marcell Dareus to Julio Jones doing one-armed pull-ups in the weight room, and Josh Chapman benching 500 pounds. I can tell him about the Scott Cochran experience and the Nick Saban experience. All of those things are going to be just such great memories that I can just sit down with and allow my son to see. Those things are going to channel his inner champion, and I think it will help him out growing up as well. I think it's going to be his focus on what he wants to be in life, and how to become a champion and prepare like a champion. I think just the whole Alabama experience has embedded that in me and I can't wait to pass it on to him.

What would you tell a young recruit who was trying to decide whether or not to go to Alabama and play for Coach Saban?

First, I would tell him that if you want to go to college and become a champion as a freshman, go to Alabama. If you want to have success in your future, go to Alabama. The script is already written for success. Alabama is always going to be on top. They've had a lot of success for so long, and it's going to continue. If you want great coaches that can help develop you into a man, let alone a great football player, Alabama is the place. If you want to go somewhere that you can give your all to the program, and the program will give it's all to you as well, go there and just allow the process to take care of itself. It's a winning process on and off the field, and it's only going to get greater.

Is there anything you want to say about the Alabama program?

I would say it's a program that's going to be there forever. The script is already written. The faces may change, but they already know what championship football is. It's going to come to a point where it's just routine where there's championship after championship after championship, just like the past when the Bear was the coach. The success isn't going to stop. For the young guys, just continue to believe in yourself and in the program because it's going to take you far in life. Coach Saban's going to help you and the staff in general is going to put you into the right position to where you're going to have success in the future.

What are you doing now in life?

Right now, I'm an assistant strength coach at South Carolina. I'm working along side of Jeff Steelman. He was recently a part of the National Championship team at Alabama. I'm just continuing to climb the ladder of this coaching carousel. My end goal is to be a running backs coach in the future. I'm just trying to be available for those who want to get better and accomplish their dreams. Before South Carolina, I was the running backs coach at IMG Academy. I had three running backs go to Division I colleges. I was there for two years, and before that I was on the 2013 National Championship team at Florida State working with running backs. I'm just following in the steps of my mentor, Burton Burns, and I just want to continue doing a good job in representing myself and my name and follow in the footsteps of Jesus Christ.

Mike McCoy

Mike McCoy is a former Crimson Tide wide receiver who was a part of the 2009 National Championship team. His high school days were spent at Northwest High School in Mississippi, where he was an All State wide out and a basketball star to boot.

Mike is now the President for the highly acclaimed Warehouse Performance Institute in Birmingham, Alabama. Before he climbed that ladder, he spent his time terrifying fellow SEC defenses with his precision route running and run blocking for Alabama. Mike was the workhorse of the 2009 National Title receiving core and he never backed down from any challenge that was placed in front of him.

One thing I pulled from this interview was how much joy Mike has for his experiences at Alabama. Mike used that joy to lead those around him to compete at their highest level while he was a part of the program. He is proof positive that the critics of Alabama are wrong in their assessment that Coach Saban forms robots that are forced to perform at his demands. Mike is willing to share with you how passionate and driven each individual member of the team is without being obligated to be that way. He loves Alabama and that's what makes his words so special.

How were you a part of the Alabama football program?

I'm originally from Mississippi. Coming out, I was one of the top wide receivers in the country. I based my decision off of Mike Shula and the receiver's coach. I made Alabama my home.

What was it like for you to be an out of state recruit and then come into Alabama? Was that a difficult transition for you?

It was definitely a culture shock. The big thing about it was that I wasn't big on college football until I started getting recruited. Truth be told, I didn't even know who Bear Bryant was until I stepped on campus. You know, I was like, "Somebody named their child *Bear*? That is crazy." (Laughs) But, when you get on campus and you meet people who already know your name before you walk in, yeah it's a culture shock. I was into a new world. I didn't know what I was getting myself into, and the experience was like no other.

What is it like for a player at Alabama to represent so many people who consider the Tide part of their identity? Was that a lot of pressure for you, or did you embrace it?

I guess with my personality I embraced it. I've always been outspoken and very charismatic. But, the culture alone… it's crazy man. I actually have some guys from the NFL that I train, like Alfred Morris, and more people are excited about Alabama players than they are NFL guys. That shows you the power of that uniform. They actually treat us like rock stars. I mean, I don't think anyone else in the country fully understands what the University of Alabama gives to their athletes as far as making them feel important and being a pillar of not only the community, but also of the state.

What was the biggest change for the Alabama program when Coach Saban came in?

Let me start off by saying that I loved both of those coaches dearly. I learned an abundance and I'm very excited and blessed to say I learned from both of them. Mike Shula was the reason why I came to Alabama. He's a mastermind as far as offense is concerned. I was sick when he left because he was the whole reason I came. When Coach Saban came in, he gave me my first opportunity to start my sophomore year. He understands the psychology and how the mind works.

It wasn't so much that he's demanding. Coach Saban asks the right questions. He'll simply ask you a yes or no question like, *"was that everything you had?"* You know, as a competitor or an athlete, when someone challenges you that way, it changes your way of thinking.

He did a lot of team bonding stuff. He knew what he wanted his goal to be. We already had great athletes, but he came in and turned that program around. You see it right now. He's one of the most successful coaches, period. That's period. He'll go down as a great.

I think Mike Shula is in the perfect position now. I was telling someone the other day that he's the only person who can coach Cam Newton, because he understands offense. But, was the transition hard? No, because everybody loved what we did. When you went to Alabama you knew you put that suit of armor on and it made it easy. It also became a job, but we loved what we did.

The first year that Coach Saban came to Alabama the expectations for him were tremendous. However, Alabama lost to Louisiana Monroe that year and a lot of people were left scratching their heads. What was the mood of the team after that loss?

Honestly, I felt like I should have gotten a few more passes that game. (Laughs) What people don't realize is that Coach Saban had a point to prove. I don't know if you guys remember but a couple of guys were suspended until halftime, and it was because of violating team rules. If he has to make a point early to get that point through, he will do just that. I guess you would say he's a mastermind when it comes to the fact that he will take a loss right now, but only to come back and succeed later.

As far as the mood of the locker room, we weren't who we thought we were. There was so much individuality on that team and I felt like after that loss we kind of started to mesh together, because that was embarrassing. But, you lick your wounds and you keep going.

In Coach Saban's second season at Alabama you guys opened up with Clemson and beat them convincingly. Did you feel like you were that good of a team, or was your performance kind of a surprise to you?

No man, we knew going into that year. That spring was just different. That year was just different. We knew what we wanted our goal to be. We were there mentally. We were all on the same page. The bigger thing was just going out there and executing. There wasn't a period in any game that we thought we were going to lose. I don't know if Coach Saban was ever scared or not during that time, but he never showed it. That's one thing he created in us. We knew if we were down, or if it was a close game, that no one could outlast us in the fourth quarter.

What do you think the fans and media don't understand about the hard work you guys put in during the off-season?

Oh my goodness. I can honestly say that the first year Coach Saban got here, that was the hardest thing I had ever done. We literally thought we were Navy Seals. There was nothing that we couldn't do. We survived!

He came in my sophomore year and that spring he literally broke us. What I mean is he ran a few guys off who didn't belong on that team. People don't realize the magnitude of it. There would be certain days we would be so nervous that most guys wouldn't even eat that day so they wouldn't throw up at practice.

People also don't realize about just being a student-athlete in general. You have to go to class all day, and then eat lunch, and then hustle over there, and then do that program, and then go to study hall after that. It's more than a 9-to-5. That's your life for four years.

As a team, what you go through, when we say blood, sweat, and tears... we were invested in it. Every year it got a little tougher, until the point of my senior year we understood that there was no one in the country who would out work us. You may be faster, and you may be quicker, and you may like it, but you will not out work us. You will simply not out work us. We had that mindset and it carried over.

Can you describe how Coach Saban uses psychology when it comes to coaching football?

Man, truth be told, now I'm my own business owner and I understand the psychological aspect of it, I understand the mental capacity of it. I guess you could say I'm in the same position now. I read a ton now. The same stuff that we are reading is difficult and the most successful people in the world understand the same things. If you want certain results, you have to ask the right questions. That's one thing about Coach Saban. He's always going to ask the right questions. How can we continue to build? Just think about it. If you've already won several National Championships, what keeps you hungry? That's something he's never lost. I was just amazed by that.

I was such a sore loser growing up that I used to get whippings when I wouldn't shake people's hands. Coach Saban, I feel like he's the same way and that's the type of guys that he recruits. You have to hate losing more than you like winning sometimes. Like, we won the National Championship against Texas in 2009 and this man was on the plane on the way back already looking at the film. That's excellence right there. I don't even know if everybody pays attention to that, but the man is sharp and he's continuing to learn.

Just look at the linebackers he's brought in. When I was there all our guys were like 255, 260, 270. And what that are they now? About 235? He understands football. The game changes. It evolves. So does his mental capacity. He puts people around him because he understands if he has better people around him it makes his job a lot easier. So, the psychological aspect of it is that he challenges us. He brings a lot of great speakers in. He makes us do a lot of team bonding. If you see one of them, you see all of them. Nobody is cliqued up, and there's no fighting going on. And then there's body language. It bleeds over into a lot. He used to always tell me, *"Mike, you act like you don't want to be here."* Like I said, I train kids now and when kids come in I recognize body language.

The things he taught us then, you don't fully understand at the time, but you understand it now. It's almost like a second parent. The same stuff that a parent would tell you, he's telling you from a different perspective. With just the mental aspect of it man, the guy is brilliant.

Since you played wide receiver at Alabama, what do you think people don't understand about that position?

I had three offensive coordinators while I was there. I had Dave Radar, Major Applewhite, and your main man, Coach Jim McElwain. Each one was very different. We went from a numbers system to just going off different concepts. With the wide receiver position people think, *"Well, if I can't play anything, I'll just play wide receiver".* No. No, no, no, no, no. In Coach Saban's system you have to know how to block. If you can't block, you will never touch that football field.

I guess my best year was my sophomore year with Major Applewhite. I loved him with everything in me. He's a great coach. You can't explain it any better than that he would throw it around. Everybody use to eat. I mean, my group would have a field day with Lane Kiffin right now. They throw it around. I don't even recognize the offense now. To answer your question though you have to learn how to block. It's a feel thing. I guess it's almost like wrestling or jujitsu. You can't look at and say, *I would do this*. It's a feel thing, and being a complete receiver isn't only about running routes and catching balls. It's about, *if I block this certain way the running back is going to cut off my back end*, or *if the safety comes down at the last minute I got force*, or *if I'm going to run a route and they bring a safety down to cover me, I have to keep this route on so the guy behind me can catch the ball*. It's a selfless position. It's a selfless *and* selfish position because most wide receivers want the ball, that's the selfish aspect. But, for the sake of the team, you have to do stuff that you don't want to do all the time. You have to be fearless going across the middle. I mean, the game is moving so fast. The receiver - I think that's the toughest position to become great at.

How did practicing against the Alabama defense prepare you for the actual game?

Man, it was easy. My nickname on the field was "Kobe." I mean, that was a name given to me by Coach Cochran because of my work ethic. We used to do releases so much against each other. There was Javier and Kareem Jackson, Marquis Johnson, Dre Kirkpatrick, and Simeon Castille. We had great defensive backs, and there were some that didn't go pro that could've played on Sundays. Going against them day in and day out made our job easy because we used to battle so much in practice that when we got in games we were ahead. Everything was full speed. Coach Saban doesn't do anything half way. There's one speed, fast. Truth be told, because as much as we use to battle in practice, it was actually tougher in practice than it was in the game.

What were some of your favorite moments while you were at Alabama? It can be personal or as a member of the team.

Personally, I would have to say my first touchdown, and also personally when I had my first 100-yard game. I guess I would say the best feeling was when we beat Florida in the SEC championship.

Do you still remember the play call for your first touchdown?

I think I was playing Z. It was a double move, Z post. I didn't even think John Parker was going to throw the ball because he normally throws to the inside receiver and I was outside wide. He finally threw it to me and I saw it in the air and it was like a dream. I mean, it happened!

Just ever experiencing a touchdown in Bryant Denny; it is exhilarating. You cannot even put it into words. Man, it's a great feeling. You know, I played pro arena ball and scored several times in there and you can't even put that on the same totem pole. There's nothing more exciting than playing in front of 100,000 people who genuinely love you. I cried like a baby my last game at Bryant Denny Stadium.

You were part of the team that broke the streak against Auburn in 2008. What was that like for you and for the program in general?

That was a situation where we just finally got that monkey off our back. It was game changing. Once we beat them we knew it was different. I can't really put it into words. It was just a great feeling once we beat those guys.

Was the focus of the 2009 team to win the National Championship?

No. Going into that year Coach Saban never once talked about winning the national title. It's one game at a time. After every win we had 24 hours to enjoy it, and then it was back to the drawing board. The end-all, be-all goal for us was to win it, and we talked about it in the locker room, but he never brought it up once.

What was your team's mindset going into the championship game against Texas?

Win. It was simply to just win.

Was it a lot of pressure since Alabama had not been on that kind of stage in nearly twenty years?

No sir, by no means whatsoever. Once we beat Florida we were just good with everything else because everybody knew we were the two juggernauts of the game. Going into that game we just knew we were going to win.

What was the experience of winning the National Championship like?

It's just different, man. You think that some kids will come to Alabama just because it's a tradition for them. Some kids will give up a scholarship to another school just to be a walk on at the University. When you're able to experience something like that, on that stage, and know that you have millions of people watching you, that's an experience like no other. That's something you can cherish the rest of your life. That's something that I can show my kids, something we as athletes can show our kids. Look what we did. We were the best team in the country that year. Period. Perfect season. That '09 team, I think we could have competed with some NFL teams.

What's it like to be part of a National Championship parade after everything has settled down?

It's so much positive energy off of one time, one town, and one community. You had people driving from out of state just to show up at the parade. I guess you can talk about it all day long, but until you are able to experience it as an athlete... I don't think I've ever felt anything like that. I think that it's life changing. Athletes are not taken for granted. I think they're very cherished here in Tuscaloosa.

Do Tide fans make playing at Alabama a special experience?

Of course man. Everybody knows what they're going to give. At the University of Alabama, you know exactly what you're getting into.

What do you think are some things that people don't understand about Coach Saban? What are some of your favorite moments with Coach Saban?

People don't realize that he is a comedian. Like, he is hilarious. He has a personality and I don't think they ever get to see it on camera because he's so serious. His nickname for me was always "Mike." I mean, I could be yelling at somebody or running my mouth like I used to and he would say, *"Mikey, I need you!"* You know, *"calm down."*

Some of the favorite moments were when we got into the locker room and he would come shake everyone's hand. And I've spent many times in his office. But, it's just a great staff. I learned a tremendous amount while I was there. I wouldn't trade my experience for anything else in the world.

Why should a wide receiver recruit consider going to Alabama over other schools?

Well, look what they're doing now as far as throwing the ball. We practice like pros. That's why the transition from Alabama to the pros is so easy. They come to Alabama and they know what they're getting.

They're getting top of the line athletes. If you go to Alabama, you have to come from a background where they work. It's blue collar, so if you want to be the best you have to be around the best. If you want more out of a career, you have to give more. That's something they do for us. They give us a tenacious attitude. They instill that in us.

How has that attitude bled over into your everyday life after you left the program?

Just an unmatched work ethic man. It's simple. Do not be out worked by anyone. If you want to be the best, you have to give the best effort.

How much does it mean to you that you were a part of the Alabama dynasty?

I think it helps me out in everything I do by just knowing the fact that I was a part of something. It gave me life-building skills that I can teach my children. You know, don't ever quit anything. Always fight to be the best that you can be. You have to have character. You have to have discipline. And you have to have a work ethic that's unmatched. So, I guess to answer that, it's a blessing that I apart of it. I can't say enough about that. I'm fortunate.

What are you doing now in life?

I'm part owner of the Warehouse Performance Institute. I'm the strength and conditioning coach.

Is there anything else you would like to add?

God bless and Roll Tide!

Lorenzo Washington

Lorenzo Washington is a former Alabama defensive lineman who was a part of the 2009 National Championship squad. He was an All-State player at Grayson High School in Georgia and he also played for Hargrave Military Academy before he transferred to the Tide.

Lorenzo was a key piece in the dominance of the 2008 and 2009 Alabama defensive line. He wreaked havoc on opposing SEC offenses. There were times, especially throughout the 2009 season, that Washington looked unstoppable. Alabama's dynasty has no doubt been built on their defensive line and its ability to stop the run. Lorenzo was one of the first prototypes of that dominance to come.

I really enjoyed speaking with Lorenzo because he carries a stern humility about himself. He is a football historian, so he understands the uniqueness of Alabama's current run. In the following interview he explains the details of what it means to be a defensive lineman under Coach Saban, and he also lays out a case for why Alabama is the greatest college football program of all time.

RIPTIDE

How were you a part of the Alabama football program?

I was a three-year starter and played on one of the National Championship teams. I was part of the recruiting class of 2004 and 2005 because I went to Hargrave. I red-shirted one year, so I was a four-year player and a three-year starter.

Because of your experience as a defensive lineman, what do you think people don't understand about playing that position at Alabama?

It's probably the least glorifying position on Saban's whole team. You know, they always talk about offensive lineman getting no glory. Well, we literally were offensive lineman for the defensive line. I mean, you had Marcell Dareus and Terrence Cody and some of the bigger names and what not, but a lot of people said we should have just played offensive line because we could move blockers and move people better than anyone else. We basically made holes for our linebackers. Basically, every good Nick Saban team is going to have a good quarterback and good defensive line. You can play with a little worse of a secondary or offensive line, but if the linebackers can't stop them, that's the whole key. Coach Saban is a defensive minded coach. You stop them and don't let them stop you. If you win 3-0, you've done your job.

What is the mentality of a defensive lineman who is part of Nick Saban's program?

Just having mental toughness and going out there and getting it. Like I said, you do whatever you've got to do. There's no substitution. There's no, "Oh, I broke a finger." You go out there and do what you've got to do. It's like a street fight out there every single play.

Since you were a part of the program when Nick Saban came to Tuscaloosa, was the switch to his way of doing things difficult for you?

I will say it was not a huge switch, because in the SEC you pretty much have to have that type of mindset. We had some good guys before me, you know, Jeremy Clark, Wallace Gilberry, and they were playing with some of the old heads, Kenny King, Kindal Moorehead, and Jarret Johnson, you know, who had some of that old-school mentality. I think the biggest thing was literally accountability. Coach Saban treated everybody - this is why Alabama players are so pro-ready - he treats eighteen-year-old boys like they can either pick up to speed or be replaced. He said that about himself; even he can be replaced.

When Coach Saban took over, could you guys tell that the power balance in the SEC had already shifted and you guys were about to start climbing up to the top?

Yeah. I always describe it as having a relationship with your father. I'm sure that you've probably gotten in a lot more trouble with your mother than you have your father. Your father probably didn't have to do a lot of disciplining. He probably just told you and you didn't want to disappoint him. With Coach Saban it kind of was like that. You know, playing at Alabama you always hear about Bear and all that type of stuff, but a lot of people realized the opportunity we had in front of us. There's not many times you have the opportunity to play for someone who can change your whole life. That's really what it was.

Everybody became much more accountable; you know, people missing class, falling asleep, not going to training, all that stuff... no. Every single person was accountable. I'm talking about the starters all the way to the walk-ons. I mean, our walk-ons doubled. Alabama has always had a strong walk-on presence. They literally were running people off from being walk-ons because we had so many people trying to do that. I just feel like everybody knew something great was about to happen and everybody wanted to be a part of it.

What do you think is something that people don't understand about Coach Saban?

I would say that he is a perfectionist. I had the opportunity to see both sides of this because I played for the Patriots as well. I'm a football historian, so I kind of see the background of where Coach Saban came from. He's a very smart guy. He has a masters in psychology so he is probably one of the most intense mental coaches, but he does it with his degree so he really knows what he's doing. Everything he does is calculated. I wouldn't say everything is premeditated because it almost sounds criminal (laughs), but for him every part of the process of the program is thought through.

I would almost say that football is 95 percent mental and 5 percent physical. He just makes you think about things and it makes you think about doing what you need to do; doing the right thing, staying accountable, doing what you're suppose to do regardless of who is there, and when that starts becoming ingrained in you it takes you into everyday life. I mean, you can just look at the graduation rates from before Coach Saban came, to after. So many of my former teammates are doing something successful. I haven't heard of too many people getting into trouble and doing anything like that. Even the ones that didn't make it through are bettering themselves. Everybody became better men.

So, Coach Saban is a master at teaching with perspective rather than using brute force to get his message across?

Oh, a hundred percent. You know, he will do his brute force. He's still an old-school coach in some ways. All the coaches are extensions of him, so he doesn't always have to be the hammer.

We always hear about the complexity of Alabama's defense, but how hard is it, really, for a player to understand?

In most levels of football, from what I've seen and playing on the professional level, they try to dumb things down. Coach Saban didn't do that. They didn't change defenses. They didn't change calls. They didn't, because if you can basically get the younger people up to speed, and make them mentally tough, they can get it, and once they get it, you know, the top already has it. Mentally knowing your plays and knowing your assignment; it goes back to a different age of football. Fifteen years ago, right before I got to college, most players didn't even start as freshmen. They didn't start as redshirt freshmen. Mental repetition was the biggest thing.

Now you have some of these amazing athletes, but sometimes because of people going to the NFL and stuff like that, you're not allowed to do that anymore. You know, our coaching staff has been amazing. Coach Bo Davis has literally, since 2007, taken basically every single defensive lineman and ingrained the technique in them that Saban wants. That's it right there. You just have to have extensions that will do what you want. Coach Saban doesn't really mess with the defensive line unless we're messing up, which was few and far between.

What is practice like during the week leading up to a big SEC game?

Man, I'll be honest. It might almost be more intense when we're playing a non-conference team, or a quote-unquote, "shoo-in" game. Basically, after Coach Saban's first year when UL Monroe upset us, we all learned really quick not to under-estimate anybody. Going into those preparations we still would do our same thing. It's mental preparation. We do the same thing every single day. That's why it becomes habit, so when we're out there and we see it we can adapt to whatever we're seeing. I mean, those big games, you could feel it. Everybody wants to play better, but you just have to treat it like every other game and do your job. As long as you're doing your job, everybody will be fine.

Could you break down what "do your job" means in Coach Saban's system?

I mean, literally, it's from day one. Like, from a Monday. If you're injured or sick, get treatment. Don't miss training table. Make sure you get your weight lifting stuff in. Make sure you go to class. You're a student-athlete. If you're not going to class you're not going to be able to play. Make sure you know your assignment. You know, that you're getting with some of the older guys that are doing some research on these teams.

Kirby Smart and all of our defensive coaches just taught us how to prepare. I mean, even the scout team guys are getting scouting reports. If the bus crashed, we could get out there with our scout team and they will know what to do. Just do everything the same.

You know, they'll throw little wrinkles in here and there because different teams run things slightly different. LSU, after Matt Flynn, started trying to run quarterback options and speed option type stuff, and the Florida Gator's with their option type stuff was a little different. Other than that, like I said, just continue to do your job. When you're out there on the field, if you're supposed to two-gap, then two-gap. If you're suppose to be a one-gap guy, then you one-gap.

So a selfish player really wouldn't fit into a Nick Saban system?

Oh no. There's not no fitting in. You would be taken off the field. Because if you don't do your job, that's how you get exposed. When you see big run plays or any big pass plays on any of these different football games in general, that's what happened. Somebody didn't do their job.

How is the Alabama program able to succeed at such a high level for so many years?

I think we just break it down from the beginning in our mental toughness in the off-season. Like the things that we do, a lot of teams don't do anymore. You know, we're running 110's and we break it down like its quarters. So we run four quarters of 110's. We treat it like a football game, you know? You treat everything like it's Game One. If you will cut a rep in the weight room, you will cut a rep out there on the football field. If you're running those sprints and you don't touch the line, everybody does another one, because out there on the field if you're over the line or to far behind the line, you get an illegal procedure penalty. If somebody jumps when you're running sprints; if somebody bends over to get water or something like that, everybody does another one. Because we're only as strong as our weakest link, and everybody has to do it together. You play as one. When you play individually, that's how you get beat.

How important has Kirby Smart been to the program?

Well, once again, any good coach can only be stretched so far. I could go down the list and show you any team that might have had a good head coach, but not great assistants. If the head coach could coach every position they would be that much better. When you start getting these dynasty-type programs, that's what happens. You get an extension of these head coaches that can do that.

Look at Bo Davis. I mean, the D line, we were to ourselves. That's what we did. Look at Lance Thompson with linebackers and Sal Sunseri when he was with the linebackers. Coach Saban was with DB's and Coach Smart was with the DB's. It's the same thing. Every single coach that coached their position could be a coordinator. Coach Davis could easily be a defensive coordinator. That's what it is. When you're a freshman or a young player you might not know everyone's job, but by my senior year I knew the linebacker's coverage. I knew what the safeties and defensive backs were doing. Once you understand what you're doing, you understand your whole job as a whole concept of the defense and that really is when stuff starts to become really good.

My senior year we went 14-0. A lot of these games weren't super close, or a lot of these games they weren't really trying to run the ball, so basically it was Marcell, Deaderick, and I out there the whole game. We would rotate and didn't have to come off the field because we understood the down and distance and we understood the schemes they were running with what they were trying to do. You know, I would put us at our strength with Marcell in the middle and me and Deaderick at our side. Whatever the game was calling for, we would just do that.

Do you have a particular moment during the 2009 season that sticks out to you?

For me personally, because I was raised in Georgia, it was the SEC championship. Beating Florida after we had lost to them the previous year, and going to the National Championship was part of achieving the goals we had set. Ironically, as a freshman, Brandon Deaderick, my roommate, said "we're going to win a National Championship," and he got into trouble for saying that as a freshman. And there we go - looking at each other like, "Man, we just won the championship!" And Georgia is home for me. I basically had a home crowd. My mom was right there in the front row. In high school our goal was the "road to the dome," because in Georgia you play the championship in the dome, so it was fitting to go back and win and go into the National Championship and win again. I'm pretty sure you can talk to most people and they will say the National Championship for us was beating Florida.

Was there any question in the 2009 defensive unit that you guys could shut Tebow down?

You know, they had great athletes and players. A lot of them are still playing in the NFL. When you watched the tape from the previous year, we didn't get physically beat. It was just that we could not stop their shovel pass the year before. We just didn't play it right. Their offense was not a true option. It's a triple option with the dive so they hand it off and they had somebody coming underneath for the shovel and they still had the quick pitch option outside. So, we just played it wrong and we focused on that.

You know, in the beginning that was something a lot of team didn't run but were starting to. After that game, we lost in the Sugar bowl and basically half of the teams we played in 2009 ran that type of offense. We just ingrained it. They ran it all spring practice. They put receivers that ran a 4.4 there and we just played the option... played the option... played the option. We just did it all day, every day.

What was the preparation like before you played Texas in the National Championship?

The biggest thing is what Coach Saban says; "It's not about what they do. It's about what we do." We just went back to the year before when we were feeling sorry for ourselves by feeling like we should have beat Florida and should have been in Miami in the National Championship. We weren't focused enough and didn't play how we should have played. We still played an okay game. We could have won, but we didn't, so all we focused on in 2009 was what can we do.

We just went out there and everybody was focused. People weren't down there in Cali trying to go out and party. It wasn't about that. It was about us coming there to do a job. "Let's do that and we can celebrate after." We've always prepared well for football games. That's like an Alabama thing. Fortunately, we have a good program. We would go out there for a minimal of five days, and when we traveled we would typically practice three days, so we're always getting adjusted to those types of deals.

I live in Texas and I believe you do too. I want to settle something once and for all. Texas fans claim that if Colt McCoy hadn't got hurt in the title game, then Texas would have beat Alabama soundly. What do you have to say about that, since you played in that game? Is that a logical thought?

No. I look at it like this. They weren't running the football on us. They're not the Texas of old. They were trying to run outside, which is because people think we're slow up front. They couldn't do that. They didn't move the ball on us with their running game all night. On run plays, the only time they had the ball on a short field in the first half was on onside kicks because they knew they couldn't move the ball on us.

Garret Gilbert was a great freshman quarterback. You know, he actually moved the ball pretty well. I think Colt would have some success as well, but with our rush out there they couldn't block us up front. We weren't really rushing or pressuring. We were just playing our normal defense and they really couldn't stop us. Offensively they did a good job of maintaining the ball. Basically it would have been a battle of the offenses. Their defense was pretty good, but we out played them on defense, and our offense kept putting up points so I think it basically would have been the same result.

For the record, the hit that Marcell Dareus laid on Colt was what took him out of the game right?

It was a clean hit. Marcel hit him good. I've seen quarterbacks get hit worse and stay in the game. A lot of people in other organizations will tell you that it more than likely was a stinger. If you look at other cut up clips from the broadcasting tape of the championship game, he was throwing the ball on the sideline. If he wanted to come back in, he could have come back in. That's all I'll say on that.

It's the National Championship game. Regardless of if you're getting drafted or not, you can only win one National Championship and it was your last game of college. Nothing would have kept me out. Josh Chapman played with a torn ACL for eight weeks his senior year. So, a little stinger did the job? I don't know how that would keep anybody out of that game.

When you won the National Championship, what was that like for you?

It was amazing. We had let out so much emotion after winning the SEC championship that we had just used it all. We were just looking at each other like, man; we're the National Champs! If we would have lost to Florida, and then still gone on to win the championship, it wouldn't have been the same. It ended the way it's suppose to - winning all the way throughout.

You went up against Mark Ingram in practice before he ever won the Heisman trophy. How good was he really? Did you guys know he was going to be that special of a player?

He just carried himself different as a freshman. He was a real serious kid. Not that he wouldn't joke around or whatever, but I don't think I've ever seen someone so passionate about everything that he did. Like, when we would do inside runs, you had to go and really wrap him up and pop him a little bit because he was always running hard and trying to run through your arm tackles. He was never trying to fumble the ball. I think I saw him fumble maybe once or twice in practice. He was harder on himself about things than any coach would be. I mean he was a great young man and that's what we needed because that class of Mark, Julio, and Marcel were the start of the younger players coming in and being very accountable. They did it in the classroom and they showed extreme maturity on the field.

I'm a top defensive lineman recruit in the country. Why should I go to Alabama and play for Coach Saban?

You will play for Coach Saban, but you have to look at the entire picture. You will play somewhere where all of your skills, as a defensive player will be utilized. I mean, Bo Davis is a quiet country boy who doesn't want the attention, but we used his same techniques in the NFL. It's just ingrained in us. There's going to be a time when a young man has to get his intangibles. You know, your work ethic and stuff is what takes you to the next level. Yes, you're going to have to compete at Alabama. You always want to go somewhere where you have to compete. You always want your bar to be hard to reach though. If you've already reached your bar, then you're not working hard enough.

How do you think being part of the Alabama football program has helped you as a person?

I think it's helped me overcome adversity. Meaning, you can look at everybody, but me specifically. We're National Champions. I didn't get drafted. I signed a free agent deal. But, it helped me in my everyday life in any type of business deal or anything like that. I know right from wrong and it made me a better man. I hope I can pass that on to any type of other players and stuff like that.

When you grow older and you can look back at this, how much will it mean to you that you were a part of this dynasty?

It's an amazing thing. You talk about looking back when I get older, but it's already been almost ten years! I mean, it's awesome be apart of something. We were the first 14-0 championship team in college football history. We were the last undefeated National Champions at the University of Alabama. So, there are a lot of records there that might not be broken.

What are you doing now in life?

I'm a finance director.

As far as your everyday job, did the tools you picked up as a player there help you be successful?

I work crazy hours. I know a lot of people would not want to do that or be able to do that, but I know with my job, it's you get out what you put into it, which directly relates to being an athlete. Every extra sprint and rep helps you. Now, only the people who are mentally strong can handle that and that's me. When stuff gets busy and people can't handle stuff and get flustered, I'm cool, calm, and collected and I handle my business. That's why I'm one of the tops in my field.

Do you have any closing remarks?

Just thanks. I'm glad to be apart of this. You know, I'm not Marcel, and obviously there are a lot of people more famous, but we're all brothers. We're all one. When we all see each other, we're all the same. We all put our hands behind the line and we're all from square one. Roll Tide.

Jalston Fowler

Jalston Fowler is former Alabama fullback who was part of the 2012 and 2013 National Championship teams. He is currently playing fullback for the Tennessee Titans and will soon once more lead the way for former Heisman Trophy winner, Derrick Henry.

Jalston was a huge part of the Riptide at Alabama. He was the fullback who blew open holes so a truck could drive through them. His opponents cringed to see him come for them head on, with or without the ball. He is known for his freakish athleticism, and his will to help his team win those titles cannot be described in the English language. He was, and is, a beast.

Jalston agreed to speak with me because he loves to talk about Alabama football and what it means to him. I think you will enjoy this interview because Jalston breaks down what a fullback goes through at Alabama, and why that position is vital to their overall success. Jalston gives the reader a deeper insight into the disciplined mindset of an Alabama player and why they have been able to win nearly ninety percent of their games throughout the last four seasons.

Jacob M. Carter

How were you a part of the Alabama football program?

I've been a part of the Alabama program as long as I can remember. Coming from high school, from the ninth grade, Coach Gary Stevenson always had me around the program, so I was around it for a while.

What years did you play at Alabama?

I was there from 2010 to 2015.

What was your position?

When I first got to Alabama I was playing running back. After that, I got moved to the defensive side. After that, a couple of guys ended up getting hurt so I moved back to running back, and I eventually ended up playing fullback.

Could you tell us a little bit about your recruitment process, and why you chose to go to Alabama?

Well, like I said, Coach Stevenson played a big role in me going to Alabama. I use to go up to Alabama to their football camps all the time. I use to just go out and have fun at the camps just playing 'Bama ball. One of the guys there picked up on it, and Coach Willis, from Auburn; he became a coach at Alabama. He started recruiting me heavy when he was at Auburn, but when he came to Alabama he kept recruiting me hard. I guess Coach Saban had a telephone call with Coach Stevenson, and Coach Saban ended up offering me a scholarship.

What was it like for you receive a scholarship offer from Alabama?

It was very exciting. Growing up I had watched Alabama. I also watched other SEC schools, but Alabama was my favorite because of my third grade teacher, Mrs. Pickens.

When you stepped on campus in 2010, was that a culture shock for you?

Yeah, it was kind of shocking, because coming from where I come from I thought I would never be where I was at. Those guys had just come off of winning a National Championship, so it was big for me. It was surreal.

Could you describe your experience there?

Oh yeah. When you first got to campus the guys just showed you around. We had like Julio Jones and those guys to show us around, and it was a lot of fun just going to parties and meeting new people. Like I said, where I came from you didn't meet new people very often. You stay in your neighborhood, and you know everybody. So, stepping out of my shell was a big, big thing for me.

Then I got around Coach Cochran. He's a guy who's going to push you and make you go harder every time you step into the weight room; trying to get you stronger, bigger, and better. I mean, just being around him makes a difference because he's gonna to push you to the max. Also, you got guys around you in the weight room who are also gonna push you to be better. If you lift this much one-year, they want you to lift more than next so they're always trying to make you better. It's a heck of a program.

What was it like for you to be part of two back-to-back National Championship teams?

Oh, that was great. I mean, the experience of the games we played in; a lot of tough games. Particularly the LSU game in 2011, and then playing them again for the National Championship. We felt like we had a lot of prove because we thought we should have won that first game earlier that year. In 2012, we lost to Texas A&M and had to come back and fight and win the rest of our games, and have a couple of things happen to even make it back to the championship. That was big. You can't put it into words how big it was.

What has the atmosphere in Tuscaloosa been like during the Alabama dynasty?

Oh, man, it's crazy. When you're winning, and playing in a big game, you can hardly hear yourself think. It gets that loud. But, if you have a bad day in Tuscaloosa, they're gonna let you know about. (Laughs) If you lose a game, they're gonna talk about it. (Laughs)

What makes the Alabama fan base the best in college football?

It's because they're very passionate about football. Football means a lot to them and even just losing a game is not Alabama's culture. They're use to winning every game and if you lose a game it's upsetting. The fans expect you to do big things every year and they live for it. They're actually diehard fans.

Was that pressure on you or did you embrace it?

I embraced it because you're either going to win or you're going to lose. You know you're going out there and giving it your all. It's like Coach Cochran and Coach Saban told us all the time that they wanna see you leave everything you got on the field, and do everything you can to help the team win.

What do you think people don't understand about Coach Saban?

People don't understand that he's a businessman. He's also a guy who likes to play and tell little jokes just to try to make people laugh. If he really likes you he will go around and tell jokes like that. That's what people don't get to see. They only see him being tough on a guy on TV, but if you get him in his office sitting down with you he's a real down to earth guy.

If you could pick a favorite game out of the 2011 and 2012 National Championship seasons, which ones would you pick?

It was the LSU game. It was a defensive battle and it could have gone either way. We had a missed field goal and they came back and kicked a field goal. That's one of the biggest games that I remember. I mean, it was loud. It was fun. It was hyped. The fans were really into it. It was a lot. That was one of the best games I've ever been apart of. The 2012 season... I would have to say the Michigan game; because that was the only game I really got play in because I got hurt that year.

What happens in the locker room after a loss at Alabama?

We just listen to Coach Saban and take in everything he has to say. Every game that I've ever been a part of that we lost he just said we have to come together and see what we did wrong. It's not about the other team. It's about us and what we did, and that's the biggest thing I take from Coach Saban. A lot of the guys come together and say we don't want to have that feeling anymore, so we push each other to go harder and be even better.

How talented of a backfield were you guys when you were at Alabama?

We were very talented because of our coach that nobody really talks about, Coach Burton Burns. He's going to make sure you have everything you're supposed to have before you leave that room. He's the one that really makes you great because he makes you study and makes you do things that are outside of the box.

When you play fullback at Alabama, what kind of mindset do you need to have?

My mindset is just go and hit the guy in front of me and move him out of the way. I always looked at it as a competition. Either you're gonna hit someone and knock them back, or if you get hit and get knocked back you lose. I always looked at it like that.

You were a versatile player at Alabama. How do you think the coaching staff was able to use you like that?

I was just a guy who could do it all. Coach Kiffin came in and saw that I could catch the ball and run the ball, and I know Coach Williams wanted me to play some tight end and up back. I really just showed my versatility in spring practice and going into the fall camp.

You were injured while you were at Alabama. Can you explain how the staff at Alabama handles an injured player?

Jeff Adams and his staff are great, man. They're one of the best medical staffs that you could be a part of. They make you come in everyday. They make you do work, and they push you hard to get you back because they know important it is to get you on the field, and they are great.

Sometimes the media portrays Alabama's program as robotic. However, you guys seem to have a lot of love for one another and a passion for the game. Could you describe that camaraderie within the program?

Everybody just loves everybody. I mean I know a guy right now who holds the team together a lot is Ryan Anderson. Even when I was there he used to have little barbecue functions and invited anybody and everybody over. I mean, then you got guys who just hang all the time. Guys just really show each other love and have fun. The chemistry is so strong it's like a family and brotherhood. You respect the coaches so much because they teach you and show you so much. I used to tell people that Alabama made me a better man. Before you leave there, you're going to become a man because they hold you accountable for everything and you can thank the coaches for that.

How much do you have to learn about the Alabama playbook and system while you're there?

Man, you have to learn everything. I mean, it requires a lot of study on both ends, offense and defense, but mostly defense. When I first got to Alabama the first thing Coach Burns ever told me to do was learn my fronts, which is the defensive fronts. Then the next thing you had to learn was how to read the safety and where the blitz is coming from. Then you had to learn how to read your holes. You can either go to A gap or B cap or C gap, and you had to know how to read the hole that you're running to. It goes really deep into detail. That's what they preach, attention to detail.

What does "attention to detail" mean?

If you're tight end is to your right and you're running a run play, and the defense is in an under, which is a one technique to the tight end side, and a five technique and a three technique and a nine technique on the backside, and if you're running a B gap play, you have to know how the one technique is gonna defend that play. Either he's gonna stay in the A gap that he's already in, or he's gonna cross the face and hit the B gap and you have to cut it back and hit the A gap on the play side or the A gap back side. I mean, it's that deep when you're playing at Alabama.

What is the leadership council at Alabama?

It's a couple of guys that Coach Saban talks to and runs things through before he makes a decision about anything. He let's the players put their input into it.

What kind of character does someone have to have to play at Alabama?

My biggest thing is to just be disciplined and listen to what Coach has to say, and try to understand what he's trying to teach you.

What kind of leader was AJ McCarron at Alabama, and how instrumental was he in winning those National Championships?

AJ was a vocal leader, and he was a leader who showed you with his play on the field. When we needed to be talked to he talked to us and let us know what was on his heart. He was just one of those guys who wanted to push everybody and make them better.

What was it like as a running back to practice against Kirby Smart's defense?

Ah man, I hated it. You got these 250-pound guys coming at you every play, and you have to pick it up. That's a headache. You got guys who are fast and can cover and come down and hit you too. I mean, that also just helps you be better.

How does that bleed over into game day?

Really, it just slows everything down. I promise you one thing, you're going to see everything in practice that you will see in the game, down to every detail. The exact way they run plays in the game will be run in practice the same way. It just slows it down, and makes you aware that this particular blitz is coming, or that particular coverage is coming, or this particular front is coming.

If you have a special individual memory at Alabama, what would that be?

I would have to say the Texas A&M game in 2013 because that was really like my first game that was just an overall good game. Then I scored what would be the game winning touchdown also.

Could you break that play down for us?

The biggest thing I remember was AJ fighting for the play. He kept saying, "We need to run this play." I don't remember what the play was called in general, but I remember AJ saying they wouldn't be looking for it. Coach listened to him, and we called the play. I remember rolling out of the backfield and being wide open for the touchdown.

Who was the team's hardest opponent while you were at Alabama?

I would have to say LSU.

If you had to persuade a young recruit to go to Alabama, what would you say to them?

I mean, Coach Saban is the GOAT, the greatest to ever coach college football. He knows what he's talking and what he's doing. You will love the campus. The guys are gonna treat you like brothers and show you around and take you under their wings. If you want an NFL caliber coach and a great staff to learn from you need to go to Alabama.

What did Nick Saban and his staff to do develop you as a person while you were there?

Like I said, they just held me accountable for everything I did. It makes you understand that you have to be held accountable for what you do; studying your playbook or what you have to do for your team. They make sure they can trust that you will do what you say you will do.

What will it mean to you as you look back and realize that you were a part of possibly the greatest run in the history of college football?

It's gonna mean a lot. I mean, I have two sons. I can take them back to Bryant Denny and show them my name on the walk of fame, and I also can take them to Denny Chimes and show that I was a team captain. I mean, it's gonna mean a lot. I can show them that, and they can show their kids that and their grandkids that. It's just amazing.

What are doing now in life?

I'm playing for the Tennessee Titans.

Did playing at Alabama prepare you well for the NFL?

Yeah, it prepared me very well. Most of the stuff we do here, we did at Alabama. I've basically seen it all and it was easy for me to pick up the offense and the speed of things once I got here because of playing at Alabama.

Parker Philpot

Parker Philpot is a former Crimson Tide defensive back who played on the 2012 and 2013 National Championship teams. He hails from Alpharetta, Georgia where he was a star player at Milton High School.

Parker walked-on for Tide, and that makes this interview one of the more unique ones in this book. He had the chance to go elsewhere, but he had a desire to play for the Tide above all else. That desire was never more evident than when Parker engulfed himself into the infamous summer workouts as soon as he stepped on campus. He never looked back.

Parker is a sharp man who carries Coach Saban's system internally. If you take anything from this interview, I hope it's the wisdom that Coach Saban is able to impart to young men like Parker when they buy into his system. Parker not only gives us insight into how that process comes to fruition, but he also takes us into the heart to the dynasty through the eyes of someone who lived it.

How were you apart of the Alabama football program?

I came out as a walk-on in 2011. So, I played for both of the National Championship teams. I played safety and corner - a defensive back.

What made you want to walk-on at Alabama?

Good question. I always wanted to play football. I wanted to come to Alabama. I had always been an Alabama fan, so I didn't really want to play anywhere else. I came there and Coach Saban was there and I wanted to play for him. It was just a great program so I wanted to just give it a shot.

Was the transition from high school football hard for you?

Uh, yeah, I definitely would say it was hard for me. You know, I had no idea what it was going to be like, and all I knew was high school football. I came on and saw the way they did things; the way they practiced; it was pretty cool. It was a cool experience.

Can you describe Nick Saban's process for us?

Yeah, it's a way you go about doing things in the daily routine. Coach Saban puts together this whole system and you have to buy in. You have to come to all of your workouts every morning and all of your meetings in the afternoon, and you have to do things the right way. You have to study and pay attention to details. They preach that a lot.

When Coach Saban says not to look at the scoreboard and instead focus on the task at hand, is that a hard mindset to adapt to?

Yeah, I mean, obviously you want win, but they did preach a lot about doing your own job. If everybody does his job, it's going to be hard not to win. Whatever position you are, if everybody does their job at that position, the way they say they want you to do it, you're going to win. You don't focus on winning. You focus on doing your job; doing the little things right.

What was the feeling heading into the 2011 National Championship season? Did that team believe it could win it all going into fall camp?

Oh yeah, I think everybody believed it. That was the goal. I mean, I always believed this team was really talented, and we had a shot to win it. If we didn't win it, it would have been a disappointment.

Some consider the 2011 defense to be one the greatest college defenses of all time.

Could you speak about their talent since you were part of it?

(Laughs) It was pretty good. Obviously, since I played there, I would think it's one of the best. But, look at the players who were on that defense. They're pretty much all in the NFL now. They were big and fast and strong. There's not really much more to say about that defense. They were really good.

Let's talk defense vs. offense in practice? Who won those internal battles 2011?

Good question. It was a little bit of both. I mean, the offense and the defense were good, so they got the best of each other at different times. It was definitely a good fight and a good thing to watch. I mean, on offense you had Trent Richardson, and on defense you had Hightower and Upshaw. Those guys are good too, so both guys won a lot.

What were your experiences like as a walk-on at Alabama?

It's all a big shock. You walk-on and go through tryouts. You work a lot with Coach Cochran, the strength and conditioning coach. Once you make it, they throw you right in and you're with the whole team. I spent a lot of time with Cochran. You know, he's a great coach and I learned a lot from him. In the meetings I worked a lot with Kirby Smart and Coach Pruitt, and those guys are great at what they do. It was really special to be able play for them. They're the best in the business. It was a great time.

What is Coach Saban like in person compared to how the media portrays him?

He's definitely intense, and he's definitely a serious guy. He smiles a lot more than what the media makes out. As far as him being intense and a perfectionist, yeah, that's how he is. He's a great guy, and tells jokes, and the media doesn't see a lot of that.

What has Coach Cochran meant to the Alabama dynasty?

I would say he's a big deal to the dynasty. The players are with Coach Cochran more than the other coaches, and it's year round. Everything you do is pretty much with him. Without him it wouldn't have been the same. A lot of the success in the dynasty is thanks to him.

Could you describe the highs and lows of the 2011 season?

Obviously the low was losing to LSU in the regular season. It was the lowest point, but at the same time everyone realized that we could be beaten. We had to press forward and look ahead. Stuff could still happen, and we could still compete for a National Championship, so that's what happened and we got to play them again. That was the high of the season, getting to play LSU in New Orleans, and getting some payback for that game. We gave it to them.

What's it like to win a National Championship?

I don't think you can put it into words. It's a surreal experience. You know, you're down there on the field and all of a sudden the confetti starts coming down, and everybody is celebrating. It's the biggest stage in college football. You work hard all year for it, and you finally win it. It feels good.

Was there a feeling of pressure to repeat going into the 2012 season?

I don't think there was much pressure to repeat. I think everyone expected it. You don't get that much time off after you win it. We won in 2011 and within a couple of weeks we're back at it; working out and getting ready for the next season. It's a non-stop process. I remember Coach Saban telling us the hardest one to win is the next one. Everyone wanted that. We wanted to go back to back.

The only loss of the 2012 season came at the hands of eventual Heisman trophy winner Johnny Manziel and Texas A&M's spread offense. Did Alabama have a hard time adjusting to the speed of that offense?

Yeah, for some reason those scrambling quarterbacks seem to give us trouble. I wouldn't say anything was different from practice. We did things the same way, and didn't switch up much. We got out there, and you get a guy like Manziel who is really talented, and he makes a difference. We just couldn't stop him.

One of the things about Alabama since Nick Saban has been there is that they hardly ever get blown out in a loss. Saying that, when Alabama was down 21-0 to A&M and y'all fought back to compete in that game, does that say more about Alabama's program than maybe all of the titles do?

I think it does. It says something about the players that are there. They are winners. They want to win. Whether they're down 21 or up 21 they're going to keep trying to come back or create a bigger lead. That's the type of player that Saban looks for. He looks for guys that are winners. Guys that will buy in. Guys who believe in the program and won't give up. It definitely says a lot about the program.

How loud is Bryant Denny Stadium on game day?

It's loud, and gets you pumped up, and get's the blood flowing. The first time it's definitely exciting because you don't know what to expect. You just follow Coach Saban out there and you have everybody screaming. There's nothing like it.

What's the pregame warm up routine consist of?

I can't remember exactly how it worked, but you go out by position. I think the kickers and stuff go out first and warm up, and then everybody goes out and warms up a little bit. You come back in, and then run back out to stretch. There's a little chart that tells you where to stand and Coach Cochran does the stretching routine with you. You do all of that and then break into individual groups for a little bit. You do all of that and then go back in one more time before you run out of the tunnel for the game. It was something like that.

If I'm a walk-on, why should I go try out at Alabama?

First, I would say if you go to Alabama, Coach Saban is going to make you a better person off and on the field. He will help you with your career after Alabama. Whether you play football or not, he's going to be there to help you. If you want to win, and compete for National Championships; if you want to play for the best in the business, and be prepared for life in whatever it is you do; that's what Alabama offers and what he will teach you. That pretty much says it all.

How does Coach Saban handle the pressure of winning year in and year out? How does he set that tone for his teams to handle it as well?

He definitely does a great job at handling that. He tries to not put a whole lot of pressure on you. He's a great leader, and he tries to get a few guys on each team to help lead the team. He tries to keep the pressure off the players, especially from the media. He tries to keep their attention off certain players. He keeps everybody's eyes on what they should be on: winning football games.

How has being a part of the Alabama dynasty changed your life?

It changed it for the better. It's something special. For the rest of my life I can say I played at Alabama and won a couple of National Championships there. It's not something a lot of people can say. Especially because I was a part of the SEC, and that's what people love. I was on one of the best teams in the SEC, with one of the best coaches in college football history. It will always be with you as long as you live.

What kind of mindset does a player need to have to succeed at Alabama?

You have to have an extremely strong mindset. You have to be tough mentally and not let your emotions get in the way. You have to be the type of guy that can handle what you go through, and be mentally tough.

Did that mental toughness bleed over into your everyday life?

Yes, I would say it does. Coach Saban preaches that. He says whatever you do in life this stuff is going to help you, and it's definitely made me mentally tougher. I handle stuff a lot better than I would have had I not ever played there. So, I'm proud I got to play there, and it helps you out the rest of your life.

Is Alabama the greatest college football program of all time?

I played there so I would say, "Yes!" (Laughs) I mean, I think we have more Championships than anyone else. Nick Saban is one the greatest coaches in college football history. Bear Bryant is one of the greatest coaches in college football history. You know, the whole program is something special. There are not many teams out there like it.

What are you doing now in life?

I've got a job with a wealth management firm. I'm a financial advisor and I love it. My job now is a job that requires mental toughness. Playing at Alabama has definitely helped me here. I don't think I would have the job I have now if I hadn't played there.

Ben Howell

Ben Howell is a former Alabama running back. He was a part of the 2009, 2011 and 2012 National Championship teams. He's from Gordo, Alabama, where he starred as a running back and linebacker for the Green Wave. Ben grew up dreaming about playing for the Crimson Tide and he eventually made that dream a reality by walking-on at Alabama in 2009. He earned a respected role on the team shortly after.

Ben Howell has an amazing story. Even the New York Times picked it up in 2012. The small town kid from Gordo, who used to look at a picture of Bryant Denny Stadium every morning when he woke up for inspiration, became a trusted member of the Alabama dynasty. He never gave up on his goals of playing for the Tide. Even when he was ignored as a walk-on he kept persevering through his passion for the game. He strapped his chinstrap tight day in and day out and helped one of the best defenses in the nation prepare for some of the best running backs in the nation.

Ben is a symbol of the heart of Alabama football. He has the "I won't be denied attitude" that every former Alabama player carries within himself. This interview is one my favorites because it shows how the dynasty has been formed through its players. Ben will inspire any football fan that anything is possible as long as you are willing to follow the system.

How were you a part of the Alabama football program?

I was a running back. I was there for four years. I walked-on so I never started any games, but my senior year I got to play some special teams and running back in some games. I had grown up in Gordo and for most of my life I was an Alabama fan. I grew up and went to games with my mom, and my dad's side of the family were Auburn fans. But I ended up being an Alabama fan. I loved it and I wanted to play there. They looked at me a little bit, but I was never a good enough athlete to get a scholarship. Coach Gentry kind of recruited me a little bit and he gave me a walk-on offer. In June of 2009 I started out up there.

What do think are some of the difficulties of playing running back at Alabama?

I'd probably say just the pounding of it. To me, the plays were easy to learn because if you're a receiver you have to learn two or three different positions like the X, Y and Z position, but the running back is just where I have to learn my position, and a lot of passing plays I had to learn protections and routes to run. The other thing is the speed of the game. A lot of the time people watch the game and think, you know, there's a hole, so just run through it. But if you don't take the right angles and stuff like that then all of a sudden there's a 240-pound linebacker in that hole. (Laughs) It's not as easy as it looks on TV or in the stands. You take a beating whether you're the starter or a back up like I was a lot of the times.

What are some of the misconceptions that maybe the fans have about the program in general?

I think people think Coach Saban is a mean guy or he doesn't laugh and stuff like that, but that's not true at all. I mean he's always a disciplined guy but at the same time he cracks a joke. He really does care about his players. I know multiple guys who he helped get jobs. You know, he told me he would help me find stuff like that. I really enjoyed playing for him because of his work ethic. He was always the first guy there everyday and probably the last one to leave. He put in the work and that's why we were so good. Another thing was when a story would come out about the team. You know something like a story about a player or something like that would come out and a lot of people would act like I knew everything about it, but I didn't know all of the details. A lot of people would know about if before I would. I guess they thought there was a lot of bickering going around which wasn't true.

How much a disciplinarian type coach is Nick Saban?

He's definitely a disciplinarian, but most coaches fall into one of two categories. You have your strict disciplinarians who are hard nosed and you're out of there, and then you have your motivators who are good at getting players ready for the games and jacked up for practice, but they may not be good disciplinarians. I thought that Coach Saban was the best of both worlds. He kept people in line. You have to do the right things if you want to play. You have to be an overall good person, but he also gave a second chance and at the same time he knew how to motivate people. He would do it for the whole team but he would also try to figure out what motivated a particular individual. In my opinion, what made him so good is his work ethic; and he's the perfect combination of a disciplinarian and a motivator.

Was it hard to be noticed as a walk-on at Alabama?

It's funny, because when I started out as a walk-on I didn't really get much attention because they were focused on the scholarship guys, but after I was able to show the coaches that I would hang around and contribute they started paying a lot more attention, especially in the weight room. For my size, pound for pound, I was one of the strongest guys on the team. I was one of the smallest guys but for my weight I could lift a lot. They could tell I worked really hard and I was dependable. I was going to go out there and know my assignment. I earned the respect of the coaches, because they were trying to figure out who is dependable. I was able to earn that because as a walk-on, you're kind of at the bottom of the totem pole. But I was able to show them that I would go out there and work hard and be dependable. That's when they started paying attention to me. I know a few other guys who were walk-ons that had that same experience as well.

Let's talk about Alabama's star talent. What do you think makes those guys stick out in a program that is already filled with so much talent?

I would probably say it's their work ethic and their want to. Julio Jones was probably the best athlete there, but at the same time I never saw him take plays off in practice or talk back to coaches. He got frustrated at times, but he never had the attitude that he was too good and I think that really separated him. He would put in extra work. Mark Ingram would do that as well. It was really just their work ethic and not feeling like they were entitled. You know, that's something Coach Saban really harped on, that we were not entitled to anything; we had to earn it. We had to earn each snap. Mark Ingram won the Heisman Trophy and the next year we didn't have as good of a year as we hoped, but he knew he still had to work hard, so those guys weren't entitled. They knew they had to put in the work no matter how much raw talent they had.

How is Coach Saban able to keep his teams hungry after having so much success on the field?

I don't know. Obviously there are some guys who do get entitled, but I don't think they turn out that great. There's a lot of guys who want to play in the NFL, but Coach would say that it's great they have that dream but the thing that is going to get you there is how you play, and how you play is how you work, and the better our team is means the better your draft stock is going to be.

He wanted us to put the team first. I felt that he didn't show bias at all when it came to playing time. You know, a lot of coaches feel obligated to do that because they might have made promises in recruiting. I didn't get recruited, but if you talked to other guys it didn't sound like he made those promises and he would give anyone a chance but you had to earn your spot and keep earning it. You weren't given anything, so there was nothing to be entitled for. There were some guys who got mad about that because they felt entitled, but they didn't make it.

Within Alabama's program how important are players like yourself in the day to day practices?

I think we're very important, especially for the defense. You know, we had to give them a really good look in practice. The better we do, the better they will do in the game. I took a lot of pride in how the defense played on Saturday because it showed that we gave them a good look in how they would react to certain plays. Obviously we were trying to play too. We didn't get to very much, but I think we were very important. Coach Saban would say at team meetings how important the scout team was, because a lot of the times, when you're not playing, it's easy to think you can coast through practice. But you can't do that, because what you do effects everybody. Football is the ultimate team sport. One cog keeps the whole machine running. It's hard to think that because know one cares about you in the media, and few people know who you are, so it can be tough. I felt like Coach Saban did a good job of letting us know that we were needed.

What is the relationship like with the starters and the back ups at Alabama? How important have those relationships been when it comes to the overall success of this dynasty?

It's important because I felt like the starters really appreciated the scout team guys. After Courtney Upshaw left he came back for the next spring game and he thanked me for how hard I worked and said it made him better. I wouldn't say I was best buddies with everybody but I had good relationships with the starters for the most part. It was a mutual respect. Football is a sport where you practice a lot more than you play, so the week's practice was the scout team guy's game. We were always trying to work hard and make the team better so when you get together in the fall camp there is a big camaraderie factor because of that work. It didn't matter if you were the Heisman Trophy winner or a scrub player.

How has Coach Saban's program helped you develop as a human being?

I would probably say it was being taught to never be satisfied. I'm already like that personally, but at the same time that showed me a lot about life. It showed me that you couldn't let up. I currently have a sales job, and after you make a big sale it's easy to try to coast a little bit, but if you do that it will affect your results down the road. It's the same way with football. I remember after we won the National Championship we got a week off. After that we were working for the next. I think Coach Saban didn't take a day off because he understood what it took to be good.

Let's be honest. You can win a championship, and no one cares the next year at Alabama. We talked about that 10-3 season, where we lost to LSU, Auburn, and South Carolina, like we didn't win a game. That's just the way it was. It was like poison in your mouth. So, it helped me take that attitude into my work life. You can take breaks but it can't be long because you have to focus on personal development and improving. That's not just for work either. I have to do that with my family and my walk with Jesus.

Why is Alabama so successful?

I think it's the work we put in the off-season. A lot of teams won't start working until after spring practice but we're hitting the weight room pretty hard soon after the season ends. Coach Cochran and the other guys do such a good job of training us. We're always searching for what we can do better. That's something Coach Saban does. He's the best coach in college football because he's willing to look at himself and change things, whether it be a routine for a bowl practice or even an offensive philosophy. He has his ways of doing things, but he's also willing to look at himself and ask if he can do it better and I think that keeps him ahead of the curve.

You're not going to stay the same. You're either going to get better or get worse, so that's something that all of the coaches do. They are always looking for ways to get better and that attitude reflects their leadership. The majority of the team buys into that and that's how we win so much, but it wasn't even about the win, it was more about doing your best on every play. If you do that you're going to win some football games.

What was it like to win a championship at Alabama? How was it to be a part of the parade and meet the President of the United States?

It was pretty awesome. I had always dreamed of that. I would think how awesome it would be to go to Alabama; to play and win a championship every year I was there. Well, I kind of fell short because we only won three. (Laughs) Obviously meeting the President is pretty cool. It was funny because the first time we went up there I was a freshman and we had beaten Texas. We went in March and the President was shaking hands and he kind of passed me. I was thinking, "Man, I missed him!" He just turned around and looked at me and told me not to worry because he would come back and shake my hand so that was pretty cool. I was just kind of blown away. To get to meet the President three different times is something I'll always remember. You know, when I got to Alabama I was thinking that I would love to play Texas and Notre Dame in a bowl game and we got to play both, so that was really exciting for me as well.

If I was a walk-on that was considering whether I should go to a smaller school or walk-on at Alabama, what would you tell me?

You kind of have to look at it and ask if you're running away from the challenge? I walked-on and didn't play much at all, but at the same time I was able to be a part of three National Championships and that's something that can't be taken away from me. Would I rather go to a D-II or D-III school and be pretty good, or go to Alabama and not play, but win? To me, it's more about winning. I had a dream that I wanted to play for Alabama. Had I not gone, and they won those championships, I probably would have regretted that decision the rest of my life. I would still have been an Alabama fan and love Alabama, but I would have known I could have been a part of that. Don't be scared off. It is tough, but at the same time go and chase your dreams.

We often hear about Alabama being a "boring dynasty" that produces robotic players. Would you like to counter that criticism by telling us how much heart you have to have to play at Alabama?

You have to have a lot of heart. Even if I had been on scholarship it still would have been really tough, because all of those guys have heart. I can think of Roy Upchurch, a few weeks before the Auburn game, giving me a ride home and being kind of down that he wasn't playing as much that year. I told him to keep his head up and his time would come and he caught the game-winning touchdown pass that year to beat Auburn. He kept working hard and even though he wasn't seeing the results he might have hoped for, he might not have been in that position if he had not kept working.

That applies to life in general. There's going to be days where you don't feel like doing things and the results aren't what you want, but you have to push through. It's no different at Alabama. It definitely takes a lot of courage and heart to play there.

Do you think Alabama will continue to have the success you experienced while you were there?

Yeah, I do. He knows how to get these great recruits and continue to develop them and have good coaches around them, so I don't see why not. I was talking to a buddy the other day about how much better the SEC has gotten and it's really because of Coach Saban and the way Alabama has made everyone else raise the bar. Once Coach Saban got there and started dominating, the other teams had to catch up. That makes it tougher but at the same time they are still chasing Alabama. Obviously he is not slowing down, but when he does decide to hang it up I think Alabama will go after another great coach.

Allen Skelton

Allen Skelton was an offensive lineman who played on the 2009 and 2011 National Championship teams. His high school days were spent at Tuscaloosa County where he became an All-State player via clearing the way and pass blocking.

Allen provides the reader with an interesting insight into the life of an offensive lineman under Nick Saban. He shows us how the process works in regards to run and pass blocking for some of the greatest backs the University has ever seen. He is a selfless person who gave his life to the Alabama program for four years without ever becoming entitled or ungrateful.

Allen is refreshment for any Alabama fan or college football fan in general. He's positive and he carries the energy that his Coach imparted to him throughout his time at Alabama. I hope that energy bleeds over onto you.

How were you a part of the Alabama football program?

I won two National Championships there. I graduated high school in the spring of 2008 and enrolled in the university in June of 2008 and was a preferred walk-on offensive lineman from June 2008 through January 2012.

Being an offensive lineman at Alabama, what kind of mindset do you have to have to play that roll at Alabama?

If you know a lot about football you understand that offensive linemen are referred to as the "big uglies." We're the guys that are on the field that don't get all the credit, and 99% of us don't want the credit. We just know we have a job to get done. We have our position we have to take care of, and we have our guys we have to take care of to be able to make the team successful. We know coming into it, we are those guys. When we are on the line of scrimmage we set the tone of every play for every game. You kind of have to go into it knowing when the ball snaps that you'll be the first one making contact. I'm the first one telling this guy, "Hey, we're here to play ball."

Let's talk about far an offensive lineman's overall goal. Alabama is known to be a power running team. How much pride (I know a lot of players on the defensive line take pride in stopping the run) did you guys take in being able to run the ball successfully against other SEC defenses?

Our biggest goal week in and week out is to keep our quarterbacks clean, but then to have a successful running game, that was our big thing. We wanted our quarterbacks safe and clean and we wanted our running backs to have at least 100 yards. We knew if we could get our running backs, especially the caliber of running backs we had while I was there, if we could get our running backs to the second level or beyond that, they would be successful. So that's where we knew if we took care of our down lineman in front of us to make contact with the linebackers then our running backs could sweep through and break open any play they wanted to.

You had an elite stable of running backs behind you for years as far as Mark Ingram and Trent Richardson and some of those guys. Is that correct?

Eddie Lacy was there too. You can also add Altee in the mix. He was a great running back as well.

How important to an offensive line is it to have a talented, yet hard-nosed runner behind them?

It means a lot to us to know that we have a guy that is, as you referred to, a hard-nosed guy. We like someone who is going to lower his shoulder and get those extra yards. If you have a guy running behind you who isn't hard nosed, then it's going to weigh on your mind a little more than if you have a guy like Trent, or Mark, or one of those guys who is going to break the arm tackles.

What do you think is something about playing on the offensive line at Alabama that the fans might not understand?

Offensive linemen really operate as a family. I played as an offensive lineman all through college and I've played on the offensive line my entire life. On every team that I've been a part of, that has been the closest knit group because we're, if you were think about it, the only group that has five men on the field every play and so we have our five guys, and we know our brother next to us. We have the same goal in mind. We have the same mindset, and we're trying to take care of the same things. We're all trying to get to the end zone. It's that family concept that you can only find inside an offensive lineman meeting room or inside an offensive lineman huddle. It's that type of stuff that most people don't see from the outside, but it makes the biggest difference in the world.

A lot of times we hear about the importance of the center position at Alabama with people such as William Vlachos, and Barrett Jones. How does the center communicate up front, and how important is that overall communication between the offensive linemen?

The communication starts with the center. The center comes up and he identifies the defense, not only for the rest of the offensive line, but also for the rest of the offense, because the quarterback and the running back are depending on that communication as well. The communication will depend on the type of protection and the type of blocking that the offensive line will do, and so as the center comes up the to the line he will define that defensive front quickly. That way the quarterback and the running back knows; "Okay this is what this defensive line is going to do, so I know what I have to do." Really and truly the offensive play starts with center. The quarterback makes the call and then the center starts off by saying, "Okay, we got a four down and we got a five down," and that tells everybody else that the guard on either side of him has this or that person to block.

RIPTIDE

As far as the SEC goes, who would you say were some of the harder teams to block during this dynasty?

LSU would probably be right up there at the top. They had a lot of defensive lineman at the time that I was there who were always weighted in the middle and they had a big guy on the nose and they had others guys that were around them that were shifty and quick. They were really hard to keep up with. Then there were times that other teams were difficult to block as well. Auburn had a team like that one year. In 2010, when they had Nick Fairley, they were tough. He was a fantastic defensive lineman to have to work against, but really year in and year out I'd say probably would say LSU was the toughest defense.

As far as your schemes up front, in layman's terms could you describe the complexity of what a blocking scheme would look like at Alabama?

We tend to run a lot of power plays, so we would have a tight end front side. We would typically have a double team block between the tight end and the front side tackle going up from the defensive end towards the outside linebacker. Then there would also be a double team between the center and - let's say the play is going to the right of the center - then he and the right guard would have a double team against that. An outside or middle linebacker would typically be picked up by a pulling guard, or another tight end/running back type player would come through to block that mike linebacker. There are many hats-on-hats from the line of scrimmage to the first five yards in order to give the running back room to see what he needs to see so he can know where he needs to go.

I want to get into some specifics. If you look at a game with Alabama's offensive lineman, a game such as the SEC championship against Georgia in 2012, do you believe that games are truly won or lost in the trenches?

Absolutely. On the offensive line, we are the first people to touch pads. They immediately set the tone for the whole game, so you're able to come up and make a difference. I would say especially in the trenches there is a lot of trash talk back and forth and you're able to come up and say, "Look, I'm here. Get ready, because you got 60 minutes of this." You're able to do that on the offensive line. It's smash mouth like that in the trenches. So, the game is truly won and lost there. You can sit down and watch it. I mean, honestly, when I watch football even today I can see it from the get go as soon as the ball is snapped. You can see that imaginary line of scrimmage and which ever way that line moves will tell you which team has the successful play on that play. More often than not if you see that line of scrimmage moving forward you know the offense is doing they're job and they're having a successful day.

As far as your experience at the University of Alabama, you were there predominately through most of the years of the first three championships. What is it like to play under coach Saban and to be a part of something that successful?

It's been fantastic. A lot more so even after football because when you're in a system that is so structured with their discipline level, then you carry that over to the classroom, and later on the workplace. You have to be successful there, but then it also carries over to the workplace. You know, you go into everything with that mindset.

When I was a senior at Alabama, and I was looking for jobs, I was going to all these job interviews and that was one of things that they asked about. They asked me how being a part of that team affected me. I was able to say I was a part of a team, specifically as an offensive lineman, so I was part of a unit that had to work together everyday. Every play on every down and in every fact had to be done together as a team and as a unit.

Outside of that there's so much more that goes into a football season and you have to have the structured discipline around that so you can make the right decisions. You had to go to class, and you had to pay attention in class. You also had to go to study hall and do everything that's asked of you. After that, you still had to go workout to maintain your body and take care of your body. You have to have that discipline to do that; and you won't do it if you don't have that instilled in you.

As far as the locker room (in the years that you were there), could you describe for the everyday fan what goes on that enables you guys to be so successful on the field?

A lot of it goes back to family. The locker room is all in order of numbers. It goes in numerical order based on your jersey number and so a lot of groups are particularly stuck together. It's like all the lockers are in a line and we're all together, all in a row, and then all the quarterbacks are together and all the tight ends are together. So you're all grouped together and you're sitting there with your brothers and y'all can all laugh and joke. It gives you time to really get to know each other a lot better than just sitting in the waiting period room, or sitting in the class room and stuff like that.

There are a lot of guys who have come into the locker room for two to three hours before practice and just started hanging out at their locker. We spent a lot of time before practice playing around, playing Ping-Pong, PlayStation, or watching T.V. We were just hanging out with our teammates because at the end of the day your teammates are your family. They are the people you are going to spend most of your time with, so the better you get along with them, the better off the team is going to be. We always had a good time in the locker room.

Of course, our being guys of 18-21 years old, we have our egos floating around and we would have competitions, and we would trash-talk each other about practice or about lifting. It would mostly be about who could do the most or who beat who at practice, or all that type of stuff. We would go back and forth with each other, but it was all in good fun because we all knew none of it was serious and we always kept it light and fun.

What was your relationship with Coach Saban like?

Coach Saban was great. I mean he knows every player individually. He has a personal relationship with every one of them. He knows us; knows us by name and he even knows our class schedules. He would come by during scrimmage when we would all be stretching on the field and he would come by and say "You had that (whatever test the other day). How did it go?" Man, how do you have time to worry about what kind of class I'm going through with how much you have on your plate? But that's just how he is. He takes a personal investment with each player.

I'll tell you a funny story. In probably about the third practice I was ever at, I was still trying to make a name for myself and was trying to make roster. We were doing warms ups and my knee braces hooked together and I tripped and fell and took out another guy. We both fell. I was embarrassed and we both jumped up and kept going and I sat down and as we were doing our own stretches and stuff Coach Saban came by and said "Hey man, I gotta ask you, where's that sniper that just shot you? I need to hide from him." He just started dying out laughing, and I was like, "Alright, well maybe I didn't embarrass myself too bad. At least he noticed me a little bit." It was just that type of stuff.

He would come around and especially during stretching and he would mess around with people and joke with everybody, but when it's time for business it's time for business and everybody knows that.

Did he ever hit you with his straw hat?

No, he never hit me with the straw hat. He did get on me a few times when he had to, but he never hit me with a straw hat.

I'm asking because I know Vinnie Sunseri was famous for saying that when Coach Saban gets on your case 'you just got Sabaned.'

Yup, in fact you can always tell when he is coming up to you and what type of interactions your going to be faced with by the straw hat. If it's on his head, your good. If it's in his hands, he's frustrated. It's going to be okay if he doesn't have the hat associated with him. If it's on the ground somewhere and he's agitated, then you're fixing to get an ear full, so you can always judge by that straw hat.

So what do you do when he doesn't wear a hat, how can you tell?

I don't know if he was ever at practice without a hat on. He always had that straw hat on.

What is a game day like as far as a big SEC venue type event? What is that like at Bryant-Denny Stadium on those days?

First off you wake up and you have your breakfast, and you have your little meetings and walk throughs. Then we all get dressed up in our suits and we go to the stadium. This is the walk of champions. Then you get to the locker room about two hours before kickoff and its all business. It's like everybody is there for a purpose, for a reason. As it gets closer to game time, you can hear the crowd getting louder and louder. You can hear all that from the locker room.

Then a few coaches will walk around and go over last minute things with their guys. For the most part, most of the guys are in their locker they have their headphones in and they're real quiet. Everybody's just keeping to themselves, getting their own mind right, and getting ready for the game. When it's game time they come out of the tunnel. If it's a night game, coming out under the lights into the crowd - there's nothing like it. You cannot beat that anywhere. There's nothing like it.

If you had to define some of the most critical moments of the dynasty that you were apart of; what were some of those moments?

I'd say probably the first big defining moment was the loss to Utah at the end of the 2008 season. We did well all throughout the year and beat so many teams, but as it got to the end of the season, especially after the loss to Florida in the SEC championship, a lot of guys kind of lost focus. We had our minds set on the National Championship and then we lost to Florida, and now we're playing in the Sugar bowl. A lot of guys lost focus and as soon as we lost that goal we had, we kind of had the expectation of, "Oh we're just playing Utah." And that whole week in New Orleans our guys took advantage of a free week's vacation and we didn't stay focused on the things we needed to stay focused on. And we got embarrassed. We got flat embarrassed.

Coming out of that game, and coming into our first meeting two weeks later, we made it a point then - that wasn't going to happen again. We were not going to be lackadaisical. We knew the type of guys we had on our team, yet we had one slip up against Florida - but that's because Florida was an excellent team. They beat us at their best and beat us at our best. We took a game off against Utah. We didn't take it serious. We vowed to each other and to coach Saban and all our individual coaches that first day back that it would not happen again. And we made sure that it didn't.

We started from day one and said, "Okay, we're going to be the best that we can. We're going to work every single day to be better than we were yesterday, and make it a point that this year if someone is going to beat us, they're going to beat us at our best. We made that decision and as a team we stuck to it. We worked extremely hard during that fourth quarter program that spring, and all through that summer we knew our purpose was to win the National Championship. We did not think anything else was acceptable, and that's the way we took it.

Another big moment was at the end of the SEC championship. Most coaches at the end of a conference championship game get dunked in Gatorade and celebrate. If you go back and look, we didn't do that at the SEC championship game because we knew we weren't finished. We didn't have anything to celebrate yet. We had another game to play. That was kind of our mindset that whole year, and it worked out for us because we knew that at our best - no one would be able to beat us. There are guys that argue to this day about what team was the best team ever, and I still maintain that it was our team. I don't think there was any team that could have beaten us except maybe the 2005 USC team, but I don't think they could have beat us either because of the talents and the mindset that we had that year.

Moving on to the next National Championship year, I think the loss against LSU was another moment. We knew we had played our hearts out in that game. I would say we made a lot of mistakes and LSU took advantage of those mistakes. In the championship we knew that we had been given another opportunity, so we were not going to let those mistakes happen again. As a team we made that pact again. That was probably the hardest loss as a player I ever experienced just because we knew that it was due to dumb mistakes on our part. A lot of people want to blame the kicking game, but it wasn't the kicking game alone. The offense also should have put them in better positions. They had to kick a lot of field goals and it wouldn't have been as issue if the offense had done their job and gotten into the end zone.

You know, it was all that type of stuff that we knew as a team we fell short in. We knew what we needed to do, so we had to straighten our act up. We also knew a lot of stuff had to happen for us to get to the big game, so we had to take care of our stuff first because if we didn't take care of our job it didn't matter what anyone else did from that point on. If we had lost one more game it wouldn't have mattered that Oklahoma State lost.

How do you think playing underneath Coach Saban and the rest of the staff changed your life personally?

It just taught me the importance of structure, of preparing, of always being ready for the next play. One thing Coach Saban always preaches to us is, "Every action always has a reaction." No matter good or bad, every action always has a reaction and so moving forward with life you have to know that no matter what you do, something is going to come from it. You have to control what you can control and make sure you make the right decisions to be able to help you in the long run. Having that structure has helped me tremendously, especially in my job, down to the point to where I'm a department leader. I'm second in command and I'm 25 years old. I'm the youngest person ever in my company to be a retail sales manager, and that has helped me to be able to have that mindset of making the right decisions. You have to know that every decision is going to have an affect on somebody else, but you also have to plan those decisions accordingly to make sure that you put yourself and your team in the best position possible to be successful.

What do you think that Coach Saban knew about you that you didn't know about yourself?

How much I really could push myself. Mentally you have your own limits, but physically there is a lot more to you. Your mind will shut down a heck of a lot sooner before your body will, and he teaches you that. Especially during the fourth quarter program all through February and the beginning of March when you're doing all the training, your mind will shut down and will tell you that you can't go any further. He teaches you that physically you have a lot more left to offer than what your mind says, so you have to be able to convince your mind otherwise, to be able to push forward and be as successful as possible.

Coach Saban has been accused in the past as not being a loyal person. Since you know him personally, would you like to address some of those criticisms?

I whole-heartedly disagree with that. Every move that he's made in his career is a move that he thought was best for himself, his family and his career. He's heavy on that. He teaches us that other people's opinions don't really matter. One of coach's biggest things he wants is for you to leave the University of Alabama a better man than when you first walked on campus. Obviously he wants us to be successful on the athletic field, in the weight room, and everywhere else; but his biggest thing is that he wants us leave as better men than when we got there. He wants to know that he developed us into good, upstanding citizens. He preaches that to us, so we understand that the stuff that these critics say is a hogwash that's created to just to get a rise out of people. I don't believe it to be true.

I know within the program a lot of people don't mention the word 'dynasty' and they focus on the task at hand. But now that you are removed from it, how special is the Alabama dynasty when we look at it through the lens of history?

You're exactly right about that. In the moment while you're there, you won't ever hear Coach Saban use the word, 'dynasty.' When I was there it was unbelievable to be a part of it because we knew as players that we were part of a great team. I don't think anybody really understood that we would be a part of something that would win National Championships three out of four years. We knew we had a great team and that we had great athletes, but we were always focused on the next play or the next game. That's how it worked.

Coach Saban preaches to us all the time that the average football play lasts seven seconds, so every play has a seven-second birth, life and death of its own. You can only control what's going on inside those seven seconds. What happened in that seven seconds will then affect what's going to happen in that next seven, and that's all you can take care of right now.

The term, 'dynasty,' was never used around there because we were always focused on who was next on the docket and who we have to play next.

Alright, just a couple of more questions. What lessons could someone like myself learn from Coach Saban's system? What's something practical that I could grab and apply to help me out in my everyday life?

Just know that whatever you do has a reaction. You have to make the best decisions for yourself and you have to know what's going on around you and be able to say, "Okay, this next step is the best step for me because in my mind I know if I do this then this should happen." You just have to focus on the task at hand, and focus on what's ahead of you. It's good to have an idea of the phrase, *"Have a 10,000-foot view,"* in the back of your mind.

You have to have goals and dreams and aspirations. It's good to have those and focus on those, but you can't achieve those goals without focusing on what's the next step right ahead of you. You can't get to step five without hitting step one first. You need to be able to know where you're going, but you have to have a plan to get there first.

What are you doing now in life?

I'm the franchise sales manager of Buffalo Rock. We're a family-owned Pepsi distributor. We're the largest family-owned Pepsi distributor in the United States. My division is out of Newman, Georgia and we cover fourteen counties. Geographically, we're the largest division of Buffalo Rock. Buffalo Rock is split into three departments. There's the operations, which is everything that goes on at the division - everything from warehouse to fleet to administration. Then there's the retail side of business which is like grocery stores, convenience stores, and everywhere you can go and buy like a case of Pepsi or just buy some off the shelf. Everything else falls under premise, which I'm the department manager for. This includes all vending, catering, special events and food service.

Do you have anything else you would like to say?

Being a part of the University of Alabama football program has blessed me tremendously and helped me in more ways than one to develop into the person that I am today. I wouldn't trade my experience there for the world. There are lots of guys that you can talk to that played for other universities, and a lot of people have similar stories, but everything is just different in the Alabama locker room. I wouldn't trade it for the world. It was an amazing experience, some of the best years of my life. I got to know a lot of amazing guys and amazing coaches.

Preston Dial

Preston Dial is former tight end/H-back that played on the 2009 National Championship team. Preston spent his prep days at UMS-Wright in Alabama. He was the top-rated tight end prospect in the state when he signed with the Crimson Tide and he systematically lived up to that hype during his time at Alabama.

Preston, as an H-back, was a key part of the Alabama offense's success. Preston did his job as a blocker and receiver for Coach Saban, and he never complained about it along the way. He also became a weapon for Greg McElroy during the 2009 and 2010 seasons. He raised the crystal ball in Pasadena and he enjoys seeing the program in the state that it's in today.

Preston is a great person to be around. He has class and shows respect towards people, even those he doesn't know. He treated me like I was a part of the Alabama program and he fully supported getting the story of the players out to the public. He did it because he claims in this interview that Alabama and Coach Saban changed his life for the better, and he wants to share that testimony with anyone who's interested in hearing it. I think you'll be amazed at how Preston sheds light into why Alabama has reached the level they have, and how it has been able to sustain it.

RIPTIDE

How were you involved with the Alabama football program?

I was working to be a member of the team. I signed with Coach Shula in 2006. Then I played in '07, '08, '09 and '10, which were obviously Coach Saban's first four years. My first National Championship came along in 2009, so that's my involvement. Growing up in Mobile, obviously Alabama was an easy choice for me, growing up an Alabama fan.

As far as the Alabama program, how would you say being a part of the Alabama program has affected your life?

On a micro-level, it's the friends that I've made. Obviously you run across some extremely motivated people all hunting for the same goal. Actually, when Coach Saban got in there and kind of unified our efforts towards, you know, understanding how to work together and all of that, we were able to all help each other win something we've always wanted our whole lives: a National Championship on one of the country's biggest scales, which is college football.

I think on a macro-level, bigger picture, the transition from football to the real world is extremely easy if you can replicate what you did at Alabama. There's a reason Coach Saban is written up by Forbes and by the New York Times and everybody else. It's because of his ability to teach people how to win, how to be successful, and not just how to be good football players. As much as we worked on being better football players, we probably worked twice as long on being better competitors, being better people, and learning how to win.

Coach Saban was not big on the word "championship" while we were there. We were more trying to *be* champions, and trying to *play* like champions. To *win* a championship, you got to win somewhere between twelve and fourteen or fifteen games. To *be* a champion, that's a mindset that you have to do every day.

What is it that Coach Saban knew about you that maybe you didn't know about yourself?

I think two things; I think he knew that I've always been a guy who's gotten along with other people - I enjoy being around people - and I think He saw my ability to lead long before I did. I didn't know what I was capable of; Coach Saban did. I think for that, he was very critical of my actions off the field as well as on them. He wanted me to represent myself and the University the right way. Him being able to understand and seek out people and capture their leadership ability is pretty cool.

As far as the position you played, just correct me if I'm wrong, a little bit of tight end and H-back?

Yeah, that's what we called it. We called it the H-back. The tight end on the end of the line is the Y, and the H is either right on the edge in the backfield, or spread out wide. I played more H than Y, but I played both of them. And that position is kind of a grinding position. It involves a lot of blocking and you will release for some passes and things like that.

What do you think about your position that maybe a fan doesn't understand?

They call it an H-Back because it's a hybrid position. It's kind of a mix between a wide receiver, a fullback, a blocking running back, a receiver, and an additional lineman. That's kind of why H-back is a hybrid. The hybrid position is interesting because you're always moving. It's not like the guard or center or tackle where you're in a set positions all of the time. You align all over the field, from outside of the wide receivers to the inside of the backfield as a running back. It's an awesome position.

I think I was lucky enough to be pretty decent at it. I think Coach Saban and a lot of those guys, like Coach Bobby Williams, helped me learn how to take ownership of that position. It's definitely, especially at University of Alabama, important. You're basically a lead blocker leading through holes, trying to seal off the line of scrimmage. The H allows the fast guys to get the edge and make explosive plays. That's it in a nutshell.

Everywhere is different. You see it at Stanford. They use something similar. It's kind of a 50/50 mix between a receiver and a blocker, but at the University of Alabama it's definitely a critical part of the running game. You've got to have somebody who can block. Obviously the guards and tackles and centers are the core of your blocking, but as much running as we do off the tackles and in between the guards and tackles, its an important position for going up to the next level and blocking the linebacker and creating explosive plays.

How important is communication between the players?

Oh, it's huge. That's something Coach Saban taught us. That is one of those things that translates into the real world and it's important in the work world too. Communication is huge. For a typical play, you've got your main play and a kind of backup play in case they've got it covered perfectly, if they're in the right defense for it. We will usually kind of switch it. We will run the other way or switch it to a pass.

When you go up to the line of scrimmage on a typical play the center and everybody runs up to the line and then they'll identify the mike linebacker, who is the middle linebacker, and all of the blocking schemes are based off of that. It's extremely important that the center identifies somebody, with the quarterback, and they agree that's the guy they want to be the linebacker that they set the play around. Obviously the center and the guard have the call and the guard will echo that to the tackle so the tackle and guard can block it together or have individual blocks. Then the tackle will echo it to the tight end and at that time the tight end will confirm that that's what they're doing, or let them know that the defense changes on the line of scrimmage.

Let's say somebody comes up on the end of the line to blitz; it's the tight ends responsibility to make sure everybody sees that coming. There's a lot that goes into that - and that's just that one run play. If it's an audible, obviously everything changes and you've got to start all over again. Communication can make or break a good team.

What do you think, along those lines, is something that fans or maybe the media doesn't understand about the Alabama football program?

I would say they're starting to understand a little more now because of social media, and the University of Alabama is doing such a good job of making the fans and the boosters feel like a they are a part of the program. I think the biggest thing is, well, two things. One, we're a family. Coach Cochran and the football team are the ones the players spend the most amount of time with. There's certain times during recruiting that the position coaches can't be around, so I think it's just a family during those times. Coach Cochran is kind of like our guidance counselor on a day-in, day-out basis.

I think Alabama fans think that talent is the biggest reason that we're winning and that we're getting the best recruits. I would disagree big time. I've been on some extremely talented teams. In 2007, there was Wallace Gilberry, Andre Smith, and DJ Hall playing. All of the guys that were on that team were talented, but we just didn't click that year. It just didn't happen.

The talent is important, but I think the biggest thing is having that family environment, and aside from the talent, we all worked harder than everybody else. I would be willing to go to any program and look any head coach in the face and argue that, because I know how hard we work. I know how hard people like myself, Greg McElroy, Rolando McClain, John Parker Wilson, Corey Reamer, Andre Smith, and Javier Arenas worked. All these guys were a part of that transitional time of the program. What we did even when we weren't allowed to be around the coaches, when we weren't allowed to practice. John Parker, myself, and Baron Huber were running routes at American Christian Academy on the weekends because we lived over there and it was a field that was close by. The amount of work we put in would blow a 40-hour workweek out of the water when it's all said and done. We did all of it so we could be great.

What is Nick Saban like in his personal time with you guys?

Obviously, Coach is a golfer and that's something I've learned to love as well. He just likes to compete, whether its playing cards with Mrs. Terry or playing golf, or whatever. He loves his family. Our personal time together was all about just having a good time. He'd have some of us over for Thanksgiving; he was just all about that family and everybody being together.

A lot of people don't think that, because they just see how he's portrayed in the media. He is addicted to success, so a lot of people think that makes him less personable, but that's not true. He's very personable, but he separates work and pleasure, big time. There's a very concrete line between having fun and working and I think the fondest times I have of Coach Saban and kind of laughing and cutting up with him is usually during stretching before practice. He'd come around and kind of lighten the mood a little bit and just make sure everybody's having a good time. He wanted everybody to share the love and the passion for the game. He did a good job of that.

When people were starting to get a little stressed, he did a great job of making sure that we kind of remembered it was a game and that we were out here to have fun, and we're extremely fortunate to be able to play the game we love for a college education.

RIPTIDE

If you had a particular game that stuck out to you during your time at Alabama, which one was the most special to you?

The South Carolina game in 2009 was one that will always stick out to me. I think the South Carolina game was the one game where I could see that our program was changing. That game could have gone either way. We went out there and we didn't play our best game, not every call worked, we didn't make every tackle, but our defense played solid and we found a way to win.

We went to the Wildcat offense and ran the hell out of the ball. It all came down to communication. They knew exactly what we were going to do, and they couldn't stop us, because we were communicating and we were all on the same page. To me, that was one of the games that we all just were all fighting for each other, and I kind of felt the program start changing then.

There are a lot of others as well. South Carolina was one that year. They had a good team, and a great defense, but we defensively just held them and stopped them every time we needed to. We also got some turnovers and forced some defensive points. We just fought together. It wasn't about who got the ball, it was just about winning.

Your interaction with the fans: Alabama fans are well known as some of the most intense fans in college football. How important were the fans to your experience as an Alabama football player?

They set Alabama apart from all the programs. I guess every program believes that about their fans, but for Alabama, it's different. It definitely has the best fans in the country. It was crazy. To walk into class and have people congratulate you after wins was awesome. They rode the wave with us. They cherished the wins and they mourned over the losses. It just makes it what it is. There's nothing like it. We would sit at the hotel, and just see thousands upon thousands upon thousands of people cheering, shaking the shakers at us, and just rooting our team on. You can just tell that a lot of these people live for those six or seven games a year at the stadium. They just take it to a whole new level. People talk about soccer Hooligan fans being passionate. The Alabama fans and the commitment and loyalty they have to that program is just mind-boggling.

Why do you think they are so committed to the program?

Well, I think its two things. One, it's the history. It's kind of like being an American. You're proud of your heritage and you have your history. From Frank Thomas to Wallace Wade and Bear Bryant, all the coaches, including Gene Stallings, were amazing. They saw a lot of great teams. I think you combine that with their pride and they're extremely proud of the University of Alabama. They're also extremely proud of the state of Alabama. I think you combine that with a state that doesn't have any professional sports; they pour all of their heart and their soul into collegiate sports. In college, there's no other football team, as far as Alabama fans are concerned, than Alabama. Its not like Tennessee, where you can also be a Titans fan, or LSU, where you can be a Saints fan too. These folks are strictly Alabama Crimson Tide football fans; I think that's what really helps separate it.

Where would you be as a person had you not been a part of Nick Saban's program?

I was lucky. I had a great high school coach, Coach Perry Curtis in Mobile, Alabama. I felt fortunate to play for Coach Shula for a while too. I think it would have taken me a lot longer to get down the stuff I'm learning now, and I've got a long way to go, but Coach Saban just gave us a roadmap to success. It just gives you a big time advantage over the competition in the world, which is everybody fighting for a job and everybody fighting for a client. To go in there and to know how to be professional, to know how to work with people, to know what real hard work is, I think, is pretty wild. I would never compare it to the respect I have for the military, but I've got a lot of military people in my family, and they're similar in the fact that when they get out of the military they understand what discipline is and they understand what time management is. I think Coach Saban gave us a taste of that.

When Alabama takes the field against an opponent, what's your mindset going into any game?

Well, it's extremely small-scale. We train ourselves to try to be as unselfish as possible. Nobody's going in there hoping to score a touchdown and nobody's in there hoping they get ten catches or ten tackles or an interception. Everybody wants to do their job and they want to do everything they can to win, but its all about getting the victory and the only way to do that is to dominate your opponent at every position.

I go in there and I know everything about the linebackers, the defensive ends, the cornerbacks, the safeties, and I know who blitzes. It's like preparing for a job or an exam. We're just so prepared because we've out-worked everybody.

I think that's why you see the confidence exuberating off of us. Everybody's so ready to do their job. They feel so prepared and that's why it comes across as confidence. Really, everybody's extremely focused and nervous and excited, just for the opportunity to be able to do their job and help the team win.

If I was a young recruit and I was considering Alabama, what would you say to me to persuade me to go there?

That's a good question. I think if a recruit wants to be a part of what I wanted to be a part of, then they should go to Alabama. I wanted to be part of the best program and I wanted to win. You only get one shot to play NCAA college football, and you've only got four years to do it. If you want to win, and more importantly than winning, to be a changed person and learn how to be a successful person, I would tell every recruit that's where they need to be. We've just proven that year in year out we will do what it takes to put ourselves in contention and to have the opportunity to be successful.

I'll tell recruits the same thing, because I've told some other people this as well; if you're afraid of having to fight to get on the field and you're afraid that you're not going to be worshipped and be the stud on the team, don't go to Alabama. Alabama is not about individual players; it's about teams. People say we've had a bunch of great Alabama players, but I'd say those great players had a bunch of great players next to them. There's some Julio Joneses that come along every once in a while, some Andre Smiths, but then there's a lot of Mark Ingrams out there too. They may have been good high school players, but they learned how to win at Alabama. They fought for their position. They became warriors at Alabama. If you're afraid to fight for what you want, then Alabama is not the place for you.

How important is the staff under Nick Saban to the overall success of the program?

Oh, it's huge. Coach Saban will tell you that, too. From Jeff Allen and Rodney Brown and everybody in the training facility, to the nutritionist, all the way up to the directors of player's development.

There are so many people that just go un-thanked daily. We wouldn't be Alabama without them. Our training staff keeps us healthy, because you're going to get banged up. The weight training coaches keep you motivated and they keep you focused on a daily basis. Obviously your position coach is with you on a daily basis as well, preparing you to be successful when your number is called.

There are just so many people who put into it; it's like a business. You've got one goal and that goal is to win. It takes a lot of people to win. It takes a lot of people to communicate and believe in the same thing. I think our staff is just unbelievable. I keep in good touch with a bunch of them like Coach Cochran and Jeff Allen. We've got some really, really good people under Coach Saban.

Do you think Alabama has stood out in this era because they go against the grain of society's pressure to promote individualism?

Yeah, I do. We're all about the team. If you don't believe it, I urge you to go to the Stadium in late July on a Friday morning and watch those guys running up and down those stadiums, carrying each other up and carrying each other down, and bleeding and puking and sweating together. You just get to a point where we work so hard that you need the people around you. At Alabama, I think we realize that. At some places they *play* football, at Alabama, we *live* it. That's the damn truth.

How special is the Alabama dynasty as far as when we look at it through the lens of the history of college football?

The way I look at it, I think its pretty special. It's an absolute blessing and privilege and I thank God daily for being able to be a part of what they're calling the current dynasty at Alabama. I was a small part of that foundation that got Alabama back on track, but in the grand scheme of things Alabama has had a history and tradition of winning and being successful and having great teams more than players, for a long time. We didn't have our first Heisman Trophy winner until Mark Ingram, my running back in 2009. But I can guarantee you there were a bunch of people before them that deserved it. It was more about the team than it was the player. It's all about teamwork.

As far as you as a person now, when you wake up every day, do you still feel a part of the program?

Yeah, I do. Coach Saban does a good job of that. I wasn't able to come this year, but he wants the guys to be a part of it so he invites the guys to come to practice. When I'm going through town, I usually go see Coach Cochran and Bobby Williams and those guys. I also will see Coach Joe Pendry. The friendships that I made on the field fighting for Alabama are still the people I'm best friends with today. I lived with Mike Johnson at one point. I talked to Greg yesterday. Mike Johnson and I are still best friends. I talk to David all the time and I talk to John Parker Wilson on a weekly basis. I talk to Corey Reamer on a weekly basis and I saw Mark Ingram last night. We all stay in pretty close touch. Dont'a Hightower is living in Franklin and I'm in Nashville, so we run into each other from time to time. It's just cool because we share that together.

If you ever don't feel part of that program all you need to do is get out to a practice in August and remember what we went through, or pull out that ring and remember all we sacrificed. I'm thankful I did it.

What are you doing now in life?

I work for a commercial real estate development company. We build shopping centers all over the country. I'm married. I met my wife my senior year at Alabama and we kept dating when I went to Detroit and played for the Lions for a little bit. Then when I got cut and came home, we started our lives together and we're expecting our first child soon. It's a boy so I'm pretty excited about that.

Congratulations!

Thank you very much.

Is there anything else you'd want to add?

Yeah, I may not know you but obviously I accepted this interview because of my passion for Alabama. I think the University of Alabama has given my family and me so much… so much. I've got memories with my mom and dad that I'll never forget and we still smile thinking about it together.

I took this interview as an opportunity to let people know that I believe in Alabama. I believe in what we're doing. I believe in the coaching staff. It's not just about football. They're changing people. They're turning people into men. Like you said, making people understand it's about the team and not about the individual.

As soon as you quit thinking about yourself, it's funny how everything else starts to play in your favor. It's a great opportunity and I'm glad I was able to share some of it with you.

Anthony Orr

Anthony Orr was a defensive lineman/linebacker on the 2011 and 2012 National Championship teams. Orr spent his younger days at Sparkman High School, where he dominated his prep competitors through power and finesse.

Orr is an example of the "never quit" attitude Coach Saban preaches to his players. He spent years inside the Alabama program, working his way up the depth chart and pushing his counterparts to improve their game with him. I really respect Anthony because of his loyalty towards Coach Saban and the whole program in general. I hope you will be imparted with some of that loyalty throughout our interview.

Jacob M. Carter

How were you a part of the Alabama football program?

I signed in 2009 and then I was gray-shirted. I ended up coming back from the 2010 to the 2015 season. I played on the defensive line and I also played at Jack linebacker.

How much of a culture shock was it for you when arrived on campus?

It kind of was. I didn't know how serious people were about Alabama football till I actually got there.

What's it like for an 18-21-year-old to play at Alabama? What is your schedule like?

It's a full schedule. You probably start out by having class at eight in the morning. In between classes you'll probably have workouts scheduled. After workouts, you'll go back to class. So you have a full day.

How professional is Nick Saban and his staff?

They're very professional. You won't find anything like it anywhere else. He's a winning coach and it shows in that he wins championships.

A lot of the players I've talked to seem to carry the same mentality. Do you think that one of the reasons Coach Saban is so successful is because of his ability to sell his mentality to his players?

Yes, it is, because he gets you prepared for life and not only football. The things you learn while you're in the program you can take with you into everyday life, even after football.

What kind of mentality do you have to have to play defense at Alabama?

You have to have a strong and willing mentality to be able to stop the run, because that's what Alabama prides itself on is being able to stop the run.

How was Alabama able to transition its defensive strategy in order to stop the spread offenses that have given it trouble in the past?

You know, on the defensive line you have your run-stoppers, but you also have your pass rushers too. There are guys who can play the inside out and the outside in, too. You have to transition to stopping a running quarterback too. When you play a team like that, that's when you can turn your defensive line loose a little bit to contain the quarterback.

RIPTIDE

Who was the toughest quarterback you guys had to go against during the Saban era?

As a team I would say Cam Newton. He was the toughest of my era, and then came Johnny Manziel.

How is Coach Saban able to get young men to buy into his system?

Well, people already know what he's capable of doing, so you have to buy into the system and what he's telling you. Once you buy into it, it's easy to adapt to what he's talking about.

Is it difficult to buy in right away?

Um, you have some people who can come in and get it right then, and for some others it takes time, but eventually you will get it, and after you get it you will be successful.

What was it like for you to be a part of the atmosphere in Alabama throughout this run?

You know, a lot of people ask me that. It's kind of hard to describe. It's an atmosphere that I wish everybody could experience. It helps you a lot in life to come from that atmosphere.

What do you think is something about yourself and the other players that maybe the fans don't understand?

It's very hard work. It's not easy. A lot of the people are on the outside looking in, but you only know if you went through that program. There was a lot of hard work put it and time dedicated.

How great are assistant coaches at Alabama?

They're really good coaches. They understand the game. They also understand the players and what to call in different situations. They know the defense inside and out.

How complex is Coach Saban's defense?

If you don't understand it, then it's complex. But once you know the key terms and the different words for the different calls, it all becomes simple for you after that. When you hear the different calls you can put it all together and know what to do. It's an NFL defense, but it's simple once you get it.

What separates Coach Saban's defense from a normal college defense?

If we're playing a team that has a lot of checks and calls, we're able to adjust to every check they make at that time before the ball is snapped. You know, we're not just in one set defense the whole time. If they make a check, we're going to make a check.

What type of communication do you guys have to have on defense before the ball is snapped?

It's very verbal. You have to listen and once you hear it you're able to adjust.

How do the "quarterbacks" of the defense make their calls during the game?

They have a play coming in and they have their checks to make. If the offense makes a check then they already know what to do. They don't have to look at the sideline.

Does that come from all of the preparation during the week leading up to the game?

Right. It comes from film study and it's all about preparation so we can do our best.

How does Coach Saban take away a team's biggest strengths, game-in and game-out?

Well, you know, he is able to slow the game down or speed it up. He can do whatever he needs to do. By him being a coach he knows what he needs to do at all levels.

Do you guys have a "no fear" mentality when you're going out to face somebody?

It's a beast mentality. When we go out there, we have to make them play our game. We're not going to play their game.

What is Nick Saban like in regards to his profession?

You know, he's very professional. He has a set schedule and does things at set times. He's the CEO of the football program and he understands how to run it and he runs it right. That's why he wins championships.

Does he enjoy his victories or is he always looking ahead to the next challenge?

He enjoys them, but during the game it's a different time. He focuses on what we need to do to win the game.

As a defensive lineman you practiced against some of the top offensive linemen at

RIPTIDE

Alabama. Who were some of the greats you went toe to toe against in practice?

You had people like Chance Warmack, D.J. Fluker, James Carpenter, and Anthony Steen. Those were all great players.

What kind of intensity do you have to bring to practice each day under Coach Saban?

You have to bring the highest level of intensity and focus because practice is going to go fast with the plays, but when you get to the game on Saturday it all slows down. That's what happens when we practice hard during the week.

When Alabama has lost during the Saban era, would you say they beat themselves or the other team gave them issues that they couldn't overcome?

I would say we beat ourselves. You know, we would go back and watch film after these games and see the mistakes that we made on each play. I think it was a matter of us beating ourselves.

How hard is it to stay hungry for success?

It's easy because you come there to win championships and to get your education, so you keep that in the back of your mind everyday and focus on your task at hand.

What were some of your favorite moments while you were at Alabama?

Well, you know, there's always the Iron Bowl and the games against LSU that came down to the wire. That's the fun part about it; being able to compete.

How tough is the SEC?

It's very tough. For the most part, the teams we played have the same type of talent but it's about who goes and executes the best. You have big guys with speed in the SEC and that's what makes it difficult.

What the biggest difference between an Alabama football player and an Alabama fan?

I guess the mindset is different. Although the fans want to win, we have a different mindset when we step into the stadium because we still have to go out there do what we have to do. I think the mindset is different because we have to play the game.

Does the high risk, high reward culture at Alabama create a lot of pressure for the players there?

There's always a little pressure but you have to be able to execute through the pressure.

How good of a job does Coach Saban do by handling that type of pressure for you guys?

He does a good job. He has different people on the staff doing different things for the players, so it's all handled very well.

How difficult is it to beat LSU in Death Valley?

You know, the thing about LSU is they have their own atmosphere there so you have to get rid of all the clutter and go out there and execute to play well.

Are you guys always trying to eliminate that outside clutter?

You have to be able to focus on one thing and that's playing the game.

What happens when players don't focus on doing their job?

You have to, because if one person breaks down it will be a touchdown.

So the margin for error is small? You can't afford to not pay attention to the details in practice or it will be exposed on the field?

Right. It will show up on Saturday.

How did it affect you personally by being a part of Coach Saban's program?

Well, you come there with a little bit of knowledge and leave there with a lot of knowledge about the game of football and life. You mature the whole time you're there.

Would you say that your pain tolerance for life rises each year you're there?

Yeah, you get use to the bangs and bruises because you practice hard everyday. That's what we do.

Do you guys take the Iron Bowl as personal as the fans?

It's always personal. It's an in-state rivalry and it's always a big game for us to perform in. Also, we want to play for our fans and our school too.

How painful was the "kick six" game for you guys?

You know, it was painful. It was like a dagger. I think everyone was just shocked in that last second, but you know we overcame that.

Would you say that the Iron Bowl is the most important game you guys play every year?

I think every game is important each and every week. We still have to go out there and execute to win. Auburn, though, is always a different type of game, especially after the *kick six* game because it added a little feel to the rivalry and it makes it a little bigger every year we play.

A lot of people doubted that the 2015 team could make a run at the National Championship after the Ole Miss loss, but you guys were still able to do it. How were you able to bounce back from that loss?

After that loss everybody had to come together and just buy in. I think that loss taught us a lesson at the same time.

Blake Sims and TJ Yeldon were a part of that team as well. How good were they as players?

Both of them are phenomenal. They are very good football players. They were a big part of our success at Alabama.

Is Blake Sims one of those players that kind of represents the entire program at Alabama?

Yes, because coming in he had a lot of battles but as the season went on Blake continued to prove himself each week.

How fast and talented is Amari Cooper in person?

He's very fast and athletic. He's one of those guys who are in the category with Julio or a player like that.

What was it like for you guys to go to the first ever College Football Playoff?

It was really exciting and we were pumped up about it. Of course, we were expecting to win the Ohio State game and go on to win it all.

How much does the SEC Championship game mean to you guys personally as players?

It means a lot because as players we know how hard the SEC as a conference is. Also, a lot of us were recruited by those other teams and to be able to go out against those team and win, you know, you got to take a lot of pride in that.

Jacob M. Carter

Does Nick Saban smile or is that a myth?

Yeah, he smiles. He will crack a smile every once in a while, especially with his coaches and players.

Are you surprised that Alabama has had so much success since Coach Saban has been there?

No, I'm not because getting recruited they tell you how the program is going to be and that you will win a championship. Everything they said about the program ended up coming true.

If I were a defensive lineman being recruited by Alabama, what would you tell me that would sway me towards picking Alabama?

I would tell you that you're going to be successful there. You're going to learn how to perfect your craft to the best of your ability. The coaches are going to get you ready to play. You know, playing on the defensive line at Alabama is hard, so anybody who likes football will want to be a part of that.

Do you think you have to be a special type of person to play at Alabama?

You have to have toughness. You have to have pride about yourself and the game to be able to go out there and do that.

How much does it mean to you that you were apart of this run?

It means a lot. It's not something everybody can say they did. A lot of people can say they went to college and played college ball, but they didn't experience what I experienced in winning National Championships and winning the number of games we did.

What are you doing now in life?

I'm working.

How have the things that Coach Saban taught you helped you in your day-to-day life at work?

It helps a lot. You know, when you get hired for a job, and people look at your resume, they understand where you came from and what program you came from, so they know he taught you something good and they're willing to hire you.

Do you think Alabama has the greatest college football program of all time?

I do. You know, I can say that because I actually experienced it. I don't think there is any other program like that. Even being recruited by other schools showed me that. You know, their facilities and the academic part and the coaches... there's nothing out there like it.

Jacob M. Carter

Keith Pugh

Keith Pugh is a former wide receiver who played on Alabama's 1978 and 1979 National Championship teams. Mr. Pugh was an important cog in Bear Bryant's wishbone offense, because he had to make key blocks and catches in order for the system to work effectively.

I wanted to interview Mr. Pugh for this book because he can provide perspective on how Alabama got to where they are today. If it weren't for the Bear Bryant era, would the University of Alabama ever have felt the pressure to hire a Nick Saban? I don't think so. In a strange way, the tradition that Mr. Pugh is a part of, also was a Riptide for the tradition we are enjoying today. Here's why.

RIPTIDE

How were you part of the Alabama Football Program?

I was recruited out of high school in 1975. I registered as a freshman at Alabama in 1976, and then in '78 and '79 I was a starter. I was backup in '77, but a starter in '78 and '79. I was a wide receiver, and those three years we won the Southeastern Conference Championship. We also won two National Championships back to back in 1978 and 1979. I was a wide receiver in the wishbone offense during those days and played for Coach Bryant. It was a great, great time in my life.

What are some things about Coach Bryant, since you played for him in person, that maybe people didn't understand him?

I think Coach Bryant was misunderstood in a lot of ways. He was a great man. He was perceived to be a very hard and gruff type person, and he was very strong with discipline, but the thing that Coach Bryant did right was that he knew his players and he loved his players. He treated each of his players like you would a child. Some children you have to spank, and some children you just have to look at to get them to respond.

Coach Bryant was a great people person. He knew how to motivate young men and he knew how to organize the staff. I think that probably his greatest strength was just dealing with people and getting the best of out his players.

I know I was not a player of great ability but I wanted to be my very best for Coach Bryant; all of us did. He knew how to get the best out of his players and to get them to play even better than they thought they could. I feel like that was probably his strength. He was a player's coach and he was a coach's coach as well. He had great staff and got the best out of those around him.

As a player who played for Coach Bryant and had a lot of success, what is it like for you to experience Alabama's modern day success?

It's a source of great satisfaction and a sense of achievement too, because Coach Saban has done a great job in recruiting and building on the Alabama tradition. That tradition started a long time before I got there in the seventies, but it also was there even before Coach Bryant. If you look at the program in the thirties and you look at the championships won over the years that Coach Bryant was there, in the fifties and the early sixties, it has been there a long time.

We began to turn the Alabama football program around by winning National Championships in the sixties and seventies and I think we laid a foundation for the current tradition at Alabama. Coach Saban has been able to come in and recruit and also build a legacy of his own. He is a tremendous coach and everybody who is here in Alabama, who are Alabama fans, are really excited.

Do you see any similarities between Coach Saban and Coach Bryant?

I see some similarities and I see some real differences as well. I think the similarities are their commitment to excellence and their commitment to win. Coach Saban is obviously a player's coach and knows how to motivate young men.

The differences I think are found in that Coach Bryant has a different personality off of the field than Coach Saban. Coach Bryant was a little more laid back in his personal life as far as off the field in dealing with people. I don't think Coach Saban knows how to relax like that. (Laughs) I'm sure he does, but we just see that other side of him. But both guys are very committed to winning and know how to get the best out of their players.

Something that is brought up a lot is the difference in college football when Coach Bryant was coaching and now. There's a big debate brewing about which era was more difficult to play in and which era brought more challenges to the table. Could you elaborate on that?

I think both eras have strength and weaknesses. Today players are so much bigger and stronger and faster, and there is much more emphasis on weight training and conditioning than when we played in the seventies. I think one of the things now the coaches have to deal with is a player coming out early for the draft. That, to me, just changed the whole nature and complexion of college football, because if you get a guy for two years, possibly three, then you're doing well. I was at Alabama for five years. I was registered then and played as a freshman on a freshman team.

You could count on your senior players back in the seventies, but you can't count on them as much now. In the seventies I felt like we played a tougher schedule. We were playing Washington, and we played Nebraska, and we played Southern Cal, and I feel like they're not doing that as much anymore. We were able to travel the country and play some of the top teams in the nation, and now with a conference with 14 teams you can't afford to play as many non-conference teams. And when you do, you need to kind of make sure you get a win. So there's a little bit of a difference there in scheduling; but football is football and it's still blocking and tackling. I think the guys today are great athletes and we had some great athletes when I was playing as well. Most of it depends on your heart and how much you want to play. We see that in both eras.

Right, and it's interesting you bring that up because that's something I wanted to touch on. It seems that if you come to Alabama to play football, one of the things you have to have is passion and heart. Coach Bryant and Coach Saban are both viewed as applying maybe a dictatorial style of coaching and some have accused Coach Saban's players as being robotic in their response to things. Would you like to touch on that as someone who played for Coach Bryant? Can you tell us how much emotion and passion went into the game outside of the X's and O's?

I think I remember Coach Bryant saying to us that football is not an easy game. If it were an easy game, then we wouldn't have enough uniforms because everybody would play. You've got to have passion and you have to be committed to football and committed to the team.

You know in Alabama, every year our goal was to win a National Championship. We knew that we weren't going to do that without a lot of commitment to work and commitment to each other to build unity and oneness on the team. I think that is important in life because it lays a foundation to be successful in life. You have to be committed and you have to be dedicated.

I think Coach Saban is doing the same thing. He's not just making good football players; he's making good men. These men will be influenced for the rest of their lives. They will be better husbands, better fathers, and better employees because they know what it's like to pay the price.

How did playing for Coach Bryant affect your life personally as a young man?

He had a tremendous impact on my life. One of the things Coach Bryant was big on was setting goals and every year our goal at Alabama was to win the National Championship, not just to have a winning season, but also to be the best. I think you can't always be the number one team or the number one employee, but you could always do your best and be the best that you can be in whatever your doing.

Like I said, whether it's at work, or at home as a husband and father, it helps to realize that nothing comes easy and you have to be committed. Coach Bryant talked about giving 110 percent, and that's what we have to do in all areas. The greatest thing I learned from Coach Bryant was that we have to be willing to work with other people and we can't do things by ourselves. As a pastor today, I see that in our church; we have to build unity and oneness and love each other and care for one another and support one another the way you do in athletics.

Was the culture of winning championships in Alabama a lot of pressure on the players when you were there? How did y'all handle that pressure and how did Coach Bryant help you handle it?

I think the pressure is a lot greater today than it was in the years that I played, primarily because we didn't have sports talk radio, and things like ESPN. The media did not play as large of a factor in sports as it does today and guys hear it whenever they drive in their car, or they see it on the T.V. as they come home to relax. There is just so much more attention placed on athletes and athletics, and I think that is where the pressure comes from.

The pressure we faced was being on the field Saturday, playing a quality opponent, and trying to beat them and being the best we could be. Of course we understood the expectation of Alabama fans is that we should be champions, and again I think that tradition is what helps us be successful. We had an expectation every year to be in contention for the Southeastern Conference Championship and the National Championship and we didn't want to settle for anything less. A lot of that pressure that we had came from ourselves, and was not external pressure.

In the 1979 championship game against Penn State you guys experienced the famous "Goal Line Stand." Fans in my generation, we see those pictures and we can go watch the film, but we really can't experience it. What was that experience like for you as a player?

That was one of the greatest experiences of my life. In those days it was hard because of the way the bowls were set up. It was hard to really have a Number 1 versus a Number 2 because conference championships were tied in. Because the SEC Champion went to the Sugar Bowl there were no guarantees we were going to play Penn State, but it just so worked out that year that they were Number 1 and we were Number 2, and the build up from the press that week was just unbelievable. Two great Coaches: Coach Bryant and Coach Paterno, two great Schools: Penn State and Alabama, the classic uniforms, everything about it just was great. We were two very classy programs.

In the week leading down before the game we did a lot of social things with Penn State and just knew they were quality players and tough players and that game was really a back and forth dog fight. They knew how to stop the ball and of course so did our defense. It was just a real tight game all the way through. It was a typical championship game where two teams just played hard-nosed football. I'll remember it the rest of my life.

Do you think that Alabama's tradition is something that makes them special, even in the modern day? Do you think that adds to the mystique of Alabama in an age of individualism?

I know it does. I think there's something today that is still as exciting to put on the Crimson Jersey as it was in my day. That's what Coach Bryant talked about a lot. Once you put on the Crimson Jersey then you're set apart. Of course we didn't have names on our back then, but the jersey really hasn't changed a lot over the last 34 years. That Crimson Jersey says a lot, not just to the players, but also to the fans. I think it also tells the country that we are the Crimson Tide, and it's an honor to put that jersey on. When you do, you want to play with pride and know that you represent a lot of people.

If there had never been Coach Bryant's era, and the standard that was set then, do you believe that the pressure would have been there for Alabama to hire someone like Nick Saban?

That's a very interesting question. I don't think the pressure would have been there to hire Coach Saban, but I think Coach Saban has been successful wherever he's been. I think he would have been successful wherever he went. I won't say he would have won four National Championships because I don't know if he would have, but I know he would be successful, because he is such a well-organized coach. I think, looking back, it's easy to see the connection there; the tradition that was laid from the teams that Coach Bryant had. Coach

Saban recruits players of great quality and guys used to want to come to Alabama because of the history, because of the mystique of the Crimson Tide. Even Coach Bryant used to tell us to come and be a part of something special. I think that attracts a lot of players that would otherwise want to go somewhere else.

So this is going to be a little bit of a trick question for you, but I have to ask it. Who do you believe is the greatest coach to ever walk the sidelines for Alabama football?

I think it is Coach Bryant, just because of the years he spent at Alabama - and I am really surprised, pleasantly surprised, that we have Coach Saban in the 10th year. When he's been at Alabama fifteen to twenty years and you see his total body of work in comparison; I've got a feeling it's going to be hard to say who was the greatest. It's going to be splitting hairs to say one was better than the other. But at this point in time I have to say Coach Bryant, just because of, not only his record, but also his legacy and what he did to turn the University of Alabama around. But again, I think Coach Saban is doing a marvelous job, but if I had to pick one right now at this point in time I would have to say Coach Bryant.

Players develop today so quickly. Did you have those type players in your day who developed as quickly?

That's an interesting question too. I think we had the talent. I think the players were capable. I think they had the athleticism. I don't know that players had the expectation to come in and play that early. Guys come in today with all the notoriety and the pressure they had at their signing day. They have press conferences and they have all the build up and they are just a little more equipped to handle the pressure than the guys who were in our era, because when you go from a high school to playing in front of 80,000 to 90,000 people - it's a big adjustment and some guys just weren't ready emotionally or mentally. I think physically they were ready, but guys today just seem to have a lot more ability to handle that type of pressure than guys in that day.

How important was it under Coach Bryant, like it is under Coach Saban, for every individual player to do their job correctly?

That's the key to teamwork. You realize that the team is only as strong as the weakest link. Every player has a job to do and it's just eleven guys giving 100 percent on every play. Coach Bryant's emphasis was you never know when a big play is going to come, and most games were decided on five or six big plays, so you've got to be giving 100 percent on every play so that you'll be ready when your time comes. We had to realize that the game could come down to something we were doing: it was a mistake or a good play that made the difference. It's just a part of teamwork in realizing that you can't do it by yourself, but you still have to do your part to make the team strong.

How much has it meant to you as the years have passed by that you were a part of something so special?

Well, it's meant a lot to me to look back. It means a lot be a part of two National Championship teams and three Conference Championship teams and to know that was a special time in my life. But the most important thing that it has done for me personally is to realize, like the Bible says, that all flesh is like the grass. In all its glory it's like the flower in the grass. It is short lived.

What I saw in football was a great experience but it taught me that the great experiences of life are going to pass and the only thing that's eternal is the Word of God and the souls of men. In my life personally, playing football at Alabama has given me a platform to share what I think is the most important message, and that is the message of the gospel of Jesus Christ. He came to save us and give us an abundant life, so I tie the two together very closely. When I think about what football meant to me, it was tremendous. But it also taught me that even when you win a National Championship, you've still got to get up the next morning and go to work. You can't live off of past glory.

If you have any advice for the modern day players at Alabama what would it be?

My advice is simply just, have no regrets. Coach Bryant used to tell us every day is the most important day so make sure you're getting better and that you're putting forwards your best effort. Have no regrets from your standpoint as far as how much effort you put into it.

I would tell them to enjoy every moment, because like I said earlier, it's going to pass by. It's football, and all of its glory will fade away. One day you'll be 34 years down the road like I am, and have a lot of good memories, but no one is going to remember who you are.

When you have an opportunity to be a part of something great like that, it is very special, but again my faith has sustained me to realize that while football is great, Jesus Christ is the one who offers us eternal life - and that's the most important thing of all.

How many yards do you think Derrick Henry would have had in your wishbone system your senior year?

(Laughs) That's a great question. You know the way Coach Bryant used running backs was different. Tony Nathan played when I played and he was probably one of the best running backs who ever played at Alabama and he ended up with probably seven or eight hundred yards with three backs getting the ball evenly. That's the reason we never had any Heisman Trophy winners until Coach Saban's era. The offensive philosophy has changed so much since then, but I'll tell you what; Derrick Henry is such a great player he would have been a great running back in any year and he would have got his share of carries, but I know he wouldn't have gotten 2,000 yards.

What is it like for you as a wide receiver who played in a run-heavy offense to see Alabama today and how they utilize these wide receivers?

As a wide receiver, I'm just thrilled for the guys now like Amari Cooper. Our whole offense was kind of centered around him his last year. Coach Kiffin has done a great job of getting the ball to our best players, and of course this past year it wasn't just Derrick Henry, but also Ridley came in there, and he's going to be an outstanding player. Again, just the whole offense philosophy has changed to spread the field out and throw the ball and there's a lot more of a short passing game.

We ran the ball to set up the pass. The thing that we had as an advantage was that most of the time we had one-on-one coverage. The wishbone, which a lot of people didn't realize, is a great passing formation because you got one-on-one matchups. Now there are so many complicated zone packages and zone coverages and things like that, but I know they're having fun and that's the main thing. The're moving the ball, and part of me would have loved to have played in that offense, to get that many opportunities. I was the second lead receiver in 1977, but I only had so many catches because we didn't throw much.

What do you think was something Coach Bryant knew about you that maybe you didn't know about yourself when you met him?

That's a great question. I think Coach Bryant demonstrated a confidence in me that I didn't have in myself to play at that level. I came from a small private school and I did have a good high school career, but people would kind of question the competition I played against. Coach Bryant saw something in me and even as a sophomore allowed me to play a good bit. He had confidence in me that I didn't have initially. Once I began to play and perform I developed into a better player. That is something that really meant a lot to me, that he would let me be a part of the team that early.

Getting back to the topic of the old versus the new era. A lot of people like to make comparisons, but as someone who played at Alabama do you see that all of you are united as one underneath the Alabama tradition?

I do, and that's another thing Coach Saban has done. He has really emphasized players from the past coming back. We have a golf tournament where we spend time together and come and spend some time with him and spend some time with some of the players he has now. He has really tried to develop a family concept and what he has built now was built on the shoulders of guys who went before.

The great thing is that you mentioned the role-players when we talked about your book. Everybody plays a role. Even if you're on a scout team, you have developed the first string. You have prepared them. When you're running the other team's offense, you're getting your team better prepared. There are a lot of heroes at Alabama and a lot of fans never know about them because those are the guys who are on the practice field, preparing the team to do their job on Saturday. They're all a part of the family.

If you were able to talk to a recruit about why they should go to Alabama and play, what would you say to persuade them?

The reason I chose Alabama, and I think this would be a key thought for any athlete who's competitive, was because Alabama is the best. There is no doubt about the tradition of the Crimson Tide and I think for an athlete today, if you want to play for the best and compete with the best, you go to Alabama. If you feel like you want to go somewhere where you can play early and maybe play more, then you go somewhere else. If you want to compete with the best and against the best, then you go to Alabama and I think that was true in my day as well.

That was my thoughts exactly coming out because I had offers from other schools, and I felt like I probably had a better chance of playing somewhere else, but I wanted to be a champion. I wanted to play for the best, so I went to Alabama.

Do you have any closing remarks?

It was a great blessing in my life to be a part of the championship teams at Alabama and to play for Coach Bryant. Being a part of the Alabama family is something that I'll treasure for the rest of my life.

Closing

I hope you walk away from this book with a better understanding of how special the Alabama dynasty really is. The players you have heard from have given us a unique understanding of the ins and outs of the program and why they're so successful. It's the undercurrent of the Riptide that has pushed everyone to greatness.

That's what Coach Saban and his staff is all about. They want everyone, from the janitor to the captain of the team, to give their all in everything they do. They teach their players to do their jobs and eliminate outside distractions. They operate with discipline and respect. They compete against themselves and don't focus on the outcome of the game before they focus in on the outcome of their individual performance. This is what sets Alabama apart from all of the other dynasties.

Each individual interview has revealed that Coach Saban has instilled that philosophy deep inside his players. It's a part of them. They've taken the lessons they were taught in Tuscaloosa into their everyday lives. They have become better people because of their time spent at the University of Alabama. The rings and titles are just a plus when you sit back and think of that. These guys didn't just play for Alabama - they truly do live it.

How can we, as fans, relate to their experiences? I believe there's a lot we can personally pull from the interviews in this book. The principles the players have laid out for us are there for anyone to grab and apply. Perhaps we also can enjoy our team with a greater joy now that we understand them a little better. I wanted this book to make all of us feel like a team together. One of the coolest things about this project was the way the players made me feel like I was a part of program and I believe they feel the same way about you.

In a way, we are all the Riptide of the Alabama program. Often the argument is made that if an individual didn't attend a certain school, then they aren't qualified to claim they are a part of that University. I disagree with that assessment. Alabama football has been a big part of my life since I was a child. It's in my blood. There are thousands of nameless faces that sit in the crowd at Bryant Denny Stadium on Saturdays who are as much a part of the University as anyone else. They spend their hard earned money on tickets. They spend their days off cheering the Tide on to victory. They talk about it at the dinner table afterwards and they share those stories with their grandchildren who will one-day cheer for Alabama as well.

That's what makes us the Riptide. We are all a silent, yet powerful current who represents the University. On a third and one, when the defense needs to make a crucial stop, rabid fans create the atmosphere for them by screaming their lungs out. At the end of a game, when a recruit is on the fence as to where he will attend school, the crowd provides him with that old tune "Rammer Jammer." Who knows how many times the fan base has swayed a recruit to attend Alabama due to their passion? Who knows how many times the Riptide has come to the shore and swept away our next star into the crimson sea? That's why we are all a part of Alabama football and its dynasty.

In closing, I hope this project has brought you some joy and sparked your passion. I hope it has kindled your desire for the Alabama program. I hope it has bred some gratefulness for how special the dynasty has been. But, most of all, I hope you can appreciate those who work hard for the program behind the scenes. Those guys give us all of their time and energy to make our lives just a little bit more fun and enjoyable during the fall. Let us honor them for their work and join in with them in the legacy they have created on behalf of the Crimson Tide.

Roll Tide Roll.

An Open Letter to Coach Saban

Coach Saban,

I'm a lifelong Alabama fan who carries the program on my sleeve. I know you don't know me, but I wanted to write you this letter to tell you how thankful I am for all of the work you have put into the program.

I realize Alabama fans can feel entitled because of the success you have created. Sometimes we become selfish and forget that you're a human being. We become obsessed with the product on the field and forget what it takes for you to produce that type of product in the first place.

I wanted to write this book, in part, to show you and the University of Alabama, that we appreciate you guys. Life is a struggle, and I guess in a small way your work provides us fans with a break from that daily grind during the fall. I know that the success we enjoy sharing has required a lot of sacrifice on your and your family's part. I know you have spent hours upon hours at the office. I know you have probably felt the pressure of being a coach at the University of Alabama. I know you have had pains and struggles all along the way. I just wanted to write you to say, "Thank you." You have brought joy into my life, and given me a small break to look forward to as well.

In a way, Coach, you're a Riptide in our lives. Your system and principles have helped improve a state that was struggling in their spirit. You have impacted so many young men who have returned the favor to those around them. I was personally impacted by talking to some of your former players. I can tell that you have made your principles a part of them. Because of that, you mean so much more to people than simple wins and losses.

Thank you for all you have done on behalf of the fans. Roll Tide.

Sincerely,

Jacob M. Carter

Jacob M. Carter

The Top 10 Moments of the Modern Alabama Dynasty:

1. November 29, 2008 - Inside a rowdy Bryant Denny Stadium, Alabama defeats Auburn 36-0. This victory ends the Tigers' six-year win streak over the Crimson Tide. Things will never be the same again.

2. December 5, 2009 - After losing in a heartbreaking fashion to Tim Tebow and the Florida Gators in 2008, the Tide finds redemption by trouncing them 32-13 in the 2009 SEC championship. Alabama running back Mark Ingram also secures the school's first ever Heisman Trophy with his gritty performance.

3. January 7, 2010 - Alabama defeats the Texas Longhorns 37-21 in the National Championship game at the Rose Bowl. This will be Nick Saban's first National Title with the Tide, and it also will birth the modern day dynasty we are enjoying today.

4. January 9, 2012 - After losing to the LSU Tigers earlier in season, Alabama redeems themselves by soundly beating them 21-0 in the National Championship in New Orleans.

5. December 1, 2012 - Alabama defeats the Georgia Bulldogs 32-28 in one of the greatest title games of the modern era (The SEC championship).

6. January 7, 2013 - Alabama smashes Notre Dame 42-14 to secure their second straight National Title. It also resulted in Alabama's third National Championship in a four-year span. Hence, the dynasty was solidified.

7. September 14, 2013 - Behind the veteran leadership of quarterback AJ McCarron, Alabama defeats the upstart Texas A&M Aggies on their own home turf 49-42.

8. November 29, 2014 - Alabama defeats Auburn in the Iron Bowl 55-44. This comeback victory was payback for the infamous "kick six" game the year before and it pushed Alabama closer towards punching their ticket to the first ever college football playoff. A week later they defeated Missouri in the SEC championship.

9. December 5, 2015 - Alabama defeats the Florida Gators 29-15 to win the SEC Championship and secure their place in the college football playoffs for the second year in a row. This was Alabama's second straight SEC championship. Alabama running back Derrick Henry solidified the school's second ever Heisman Trophy by rushing for 189 yards against one of the nation's top defenses.

10. January 11, 2016 - Alabama defeats the Clemson Tigers 45-40 to win their first ever college football playoff National Title. This was Alabama's fourth National Championship in seven years and it secured Alabama's spot as one the greatest dynasties the sports world has ever seen.

Jacob M. Carter

Is Alabama a dynasty?

By definition, a sports dynasty is a made up of a team who dominates their league for an extraordinary length of time. Alabama has certainly done that. From the good ol' days of Bear Bryant to the modern days of Nick Saban, Alabama has won an astonishing amount of championships - 16 in all!

In the modern era the Crimson Tide has won four National Championships over the span of seven years – capturing the National Title in 2009, 2011, 2012 and 2015. Since 2009 Alabama has a record of 86 wins vs 10 losses, earning four SEC titles along with their four National Titles. They finished in the Top 5 rankings five times during that period. Oh yeah, they also had two players win the coveted Heisman Trophy: RB Mark Ingram in 2009 and RB Derrick Henry in 2015.

What's even more significant about the dynasty is that they have dominated the college scene during a time of difficult competition and social media exposure. Recruiting is a trying task these days with all of the attention that each individual prep star receives. Schools can come at kids when they are a young as 12-years-old and this has created a new challenge for sacred cowl schools like Alabama.

Alabama has won games at a consistently high level in one of the hardest conferences in college football, the Southeastern Conference. Week in and week out they have lined up against some of the most physical teams in the country. It seems like Alabama has five or six primetime games a season.

When you add all of those factors together it's easy to see why Alabama deserves the title of being a dynasty.

Last season Alabama proved they could continue to succeed by winning their first ever College Football Playoff Championship. That win only further solidified their place as the greatest college football dynasty ever.

RIPTIDE

What will the future hold for the Crimson Tide? By the looks of it, the future is bright. Coach Saban still has the fire to train young men till they become great leaders on and off the field, and these young men still happen to be highly sought after recruits. The combustion of the tradition at Alabama and the pressure to win has created a run that will likely never be matched again. I could see Alabama winning it all again... and again... if this process continues according to plan.

Jacob M. Carter

Thoughts on the After Life

Alabama football is a successful program. There's no doubt about it. Stored inside their museums and decorated halls are piles of trophies, mementos and awards. They have had two of the greatest coaches in college football history. They are praised for their undying dedication to their craft and they are worthy of that praise due to their driven nature, and their obvious results.

However, as a Christian man, I hope we can take some time to look past those accomplishments and refocus our gaze towards the final goal in life - the judgment seat of Christ.

Six years ago, I was drowning in a severe drug addiction and I couldn't find any way out. I was lost in my sin. That is when the Lord intervened in my life. He poured His grace into my soul and He opened my eyes so I could see the value of His Son's sacrifice on the cross. I was crushed by the realization that everything I was pursuing in this world was meaningless if I were to lose my soul. This realization drove me into Christ's open arms. He saved me from myself and I've never been the same since.

After my salvation, my worldview changed. I no longer saw the pursuits of the world as the end-all of life. Trophies and accolades are a great thing to strive for on this side of eternity, but we won't take them with us when we stand in front of the Almighty. The only question on that Day will be, What is the state of your soul? Were you saved by Christ and His righteousness? Was He the Lord of your life while you walked on this earth? Did you deny yourself and take up your cross to follow Him, no matter the cost? There will be no mention of what we accomplished in this world or what we were able to do with our abilities outside of Christ. The only question will revolve around God's Word and how that Word changed our hearts.

I'm an Alabama fan, so I understand the fanaticism that comes with being a part of the program. I want the Tide to win as badly as anyone else does, and I enjoy the heck out of it when they do. However, my hope is not ultimately in the football program.

All things, as Mr. Pugh reminded us, will pass away. In light of that I hope that everyone who reads this book will shift their perspective on what is important in life and what isn't. I pray that the Gospel will penetrate our hearts and drive us to repentance before God if we are more consumed with this world than we are about the next. God has given us many graces, and football, I believe, is one of them. Let us enjoy his gifts and give Him praise for them daily. Yet, let us also never forget to set our eyes on the only prize that truly matters: The gift of salvation, by placing our faith in Christ's life, death, and resurrection.

In love,

Jacob M. Carter

The RipTide in My Life

Just as the Alabama program has a riptide behind all of its success, so do I. I want to thank all of them.

My mother never gave up on me and she deserves all of the credit in the world for her unconditional love during crucial times in my life. I love you mom. My Pastor, Pete Orta, and his wife, Kelli Orta, and their kids, Dorian, Jett, Keen and Zade, and their grandmother, Jo, have sacrificed so much of their personal life so I could have one of my own. I will never be able to repay the love they have shown me because their love was genuine. I love all of you from the bottom of my heart. My teachers encouraged me to write along the way. Your lessons have stuck with me. Darrian Howard allowed me to use his recorder for the interviews in this book. Thanks bro! The guys at In Triumph stepped in for me on my duties when I needed to complete an interview. You guys make me so proud and I love to see the growth in your life. My church family at Bema Church have made my life a joy and I'm so fortunate to have them in my life. You mean so much to me. My publishers, Mike and Paula Parker, for their commitment to my work. You guys took a chance on me when nobody else would. I hope I make you guys proud and I'm so thankful for the work you put in on my behalf. The players I interviewed for this book were amazing. You guys are the reason the Alabama program is at the level it is. I was truly impressed by your character and passion. Eric Hudson, my childhood friend and brother, encouraged me to start this project and he deserves a lot of credit for his fingerprints on this book. Gayle Talabay and Deanna Waller spent their personal time transcribing some interviews for me so I could spend more time on my writing. You guys are the best. Drew DeArmond gave me advice about reaching players early on and I want to thank him as well. If there is anyone else I'm missing, please forgive me. I have nothing but admiration for all of the undercurrents in my life.

Also Available From

WordCrafts Press

Before History Dies
   by Jacob M. Carter

Never Run a Dead Kata
   by Rodney Boyd

Aerobics for the Mind
   by Michael Potts, PhD

Why I Failed in the Music Business
      and how NOT to follow in my footsteps
   by Steve Grossman

Letters at Midnight
   by Roland B. King

Uncommon Core
   by Pauline Hawkins

Shameless Self Promotion
   by Parker, Parker & Martin

A Scarlet Cord of Hope
   By Sheryl Griffin

CPSIA information can be obtained
at www.ICGtesting.com
Printed in the USA
LVOW10s0230261017
553825LV00024B/925/P